Mindfulness for
Anger Management

Mindfulness for Anger Management

Transformative Skills for Overcoming Anger and Managing Powerful Emotions

Stephen Dansiger, PsyD, MFT

ALTHEA
PRESS

Interior Designer: Liz Cosgrove
Cover Designer: Amy King
Photo Art Director: Amy Hartmann
Editor: Melissa Valentine
Production Editor: Andrew Yackira

Cover illustration: Artishokcs/iStock.com. Interior illustration: Flas100/shutterstock.com.
Author photo courtesy of Gen Max

ISBN: Print 978-1-64152-167-3 | eBook 978-1-64152-168-0

To all those actively engaged in ending suffering
and the causes of suffering.

Contents

Introduction

ANGER. The word has a very bad reputation, and with good reason. Many of us have seen it destroy a moment in time, or a day, or even a life. It is seen as a poison by a number of spiritual and religious traditions, and it fuels all manner of hurtful behavior. But as John Lydon of Public Image Ltd chanted over and again in his song "Rise":

"Anger is an energy!"

This book will help you retool that energy, see it for what it is, and allow you to manage anger and other difficult emotions. One major way we will accomplish that together is by deeply investigating the true nature of anger. The energy that manifests as anger has many components. There is the biology of fight or flight and the incredible brain and body changes that come with that survival instinct. There is the psychology of right and wrong, my way or the highway, justice and injustice, and all other binary distinctions that bring conflict. There is the misunderstanding of anger as being only about rage and acting out that rage. The truth is that anger involves a continuum of human emotion and experience. When we understand that deeply, we are able to address all the elements of that continuum in order to come up with the best anger management plan.

Mindfulness, a best practice devised almost 2,600 years ago in the north of India, is a key tool for investigating anger as a component of our entire emotional experience. In the simplest terms, mindfulness is a way of directing attention onto an experience and, in doing so, developing a nonjudgmental distance from it as separate from you. Buddha and those who have taught mindfulness over the following millennia found that anger and its related emotions–those considered undesirable or negative–are in fact an integral part of the human experience and equally deserving of our attention and investigation. He found that if we turn *toward* these emotions rather than running away from them, if we place mindful attention upon them with an attitude of kindness, this seemingly counterintuitive move will bring an end to our suffering. In this case, ending suffering means bringing an end to being dominated and led by our intense emotions, and instead letting them exist without disrupting our well-being.

So, as we develop a plan for this powerful emotion known as anger, the central guiding question becomes: How do we turn our gaze *toward* anger and other strong emotions without becoming swept away by them and their accompanying thoughts, feelings, and body sensations? This book is designed to reveal the answer to that question.

As we walk together through this process, you will learn basic and more advanced mindfulness skills. As we go along, the initial skills of simply noticing your experience will help you get some immediate symptom relief, whether your symptoms are resentment, depression, anxiety, or other problems related to anger. You will also be building the foundation of a long-term anger management strategy that is unique to your circumstances. This will be facilitated by having a variety of strategies to choose from, starting with simply counting your way through a moment to meditations on self-compassion and loving-kindness. Whether your symptoms are bouts of rage, anger at yourself, an inability to feel your own anger, or anything in between, the skills in this book will help.

As your guide through this process, I am committed to openness regarding all my experiences, including my years as an angry young person, my awakening to the power of my own anger, and my anger recovery. I also look forward to sharing with you my own 30 years of active mindfulness practice, including 25 years of teaching mindfulness, running anger management groups, and working with individuals on their own anger-related issues. For me, the answer has always been grounded in mindfulness. I look forward to walking with you, shoulder to shoulder, into a new life filled with more peace, focus, and a new feeling of agency over your emotional life.

I grew up in a family where only the adults were allowed to express their anger. Other people with the same experience rebelled and fought back. In my case, my small stature had me go toward repressing my anger throughout my childhood and into my teens. I found that alcohol and other substances reduced my inhibitions, and once I began to use those substances, those around me found out about my anger. When I got sober at 26, my anger bubbled up again without the availability of my usual coping mechanism. I got involved in 12-step recovery and learned that these fellowships are actually anger management programs—investigations into one's resentments and entrenched anger. By turning mindfully toward these resentments, healing is experienced.

Early in my recovery, I was brought to a 12-step retreat at a Zen Buddhist monastery, and I received my first mindfulness training. I have maintained an ongoing mediation practice for nearly 30 years. My first major challenge was at work, when I became a high school English teacher, and my mindfulness and anger management skills were put to the test daily. When racially motivated riots broke out near the school, I was trained to help people understand and begin healing those anger-driven wounds, and within a short period of time, I was thrust personally and professionally into mindfulness-based anger management.

After years as an educator and musician, I became a psychotherapist. Specifically, an EMDR (Eye Movement Desensitization Reprocessing) therapist. This powerful therapy is known for being a best practice, evidence-based treatment for post-traumatic stress disorder (PTSD). The most important thing I have learned from working with EMDR is that a majority of our ills come from maladaptively processed memories. This is not just about trauma but adverse life events—anything that rubs us the wrong way, anything that might trigger anger. These events or phases in our life where the information does not make it to the smart part of our brain remain stuck in the feeling center of our brain. This makes us susceptible to running our life on our feelings alone, and when anger is featured, chaos can ensue. Through working on my own issues and those of my clients in this manner, I have found that these strong feelings can be our allies and we absolutely possess the ability to bring them to a mindful resolution. My 12-step work, my work as an educator, and my work as an EMDR therapist have made it clear that managing my anger is not just about averting disaster; it is about infinitely improving my quality of life—both inside and out.

My life has been quite remarkable as a result. Today, anger is not what runs my life. I am able to be a spouse, a parent, a community member, a therapist, and a creative person. I am able to fully integrate the strong feelings associated with anger and not act on them in a harmful way. I have found that teaching the skills in this book to my clients helps them do the same.

People who came to me with house arrest ankle bracelets because someone cut them off on the highway are now living peacefully among their families and communities.

People who raged at family members now communicate constructively.

People whose rage turned inward now find compassion for themselves, leading to constructive and healthy expression of their feelings of anger.

People who could set boundaries only through acting on anger physically or verbally are now able to set healthy boundaries that are not driven completely by fight or flight.

Whatever anger dilemma brought you to this book, the development of these mindfulness skills can help you meet your goals. I have seen it time after time in my own life and in the lives of those I work with on these issues. I want to see the same for you.

How to Use This Book

I want you to understand that mindfulness works. It really does. But mindfulness is a skill, and just as with any other skill, it grows stronger over time and with practice. Anger management is not always going to be an instant gratification game. We have lived with and will continue to live with this emotion throughout our lives, so bringing it into awareness and dealing with it in a way that is effective will also be a lifelong journey. However, if you do make a commitment to this framework of mindfulness-based anger management, you will notice subtle (and sometimes not so subtle) changes in the way you experience your anger and the way you act on it or don't act on it. I encourage you to work with the skills you learn in this book every day to fully benefit from a truly transformed relationship to your anger.

Throughout the book there will be real-life anecdotes about how people have been affected by their anger and general examples of how mindfulness and other psychological strategies have helped them think, feel, and act differently. Anger manifests differently for different people. Wherever you fall on the continuum of anger strategies and styles, try to see how each example can help you understand the journey from anger that is or seems out of control to anger understood and managed.

In order for us to work with anger, we need a deeper understanding of it. We will explore the foundations of our anger, the purpose of anger, and the wonderful possibilities of applying mindfulness to anger in order for it to become a useful energy that we can use on behalf of ourselves and others.

PART ONE

UNDERSTANDING ANGER

Anger is a basic universal emotion, as common as happiness and sadness. It's a natural response to stress or frustration and can actually be beneficial if we relate to it in a healthy way. This section takes a look at the various ways anger presents and becomes problematic. We'll also learn about mindfulness, a transformative skill set and mindset that will help you relate to your anger in new ways.

CHAPTER 1

What Is Anger?

Anger has a bad reputation among the emotions, but it is a normal and often healthy emotion. Most other emotions have not had books written about them with the word *management* in the title...for instance, *Joy Management* has not hit the shelves of your local independent bookstore (although a case could be made for why it should). Strong emotions are indicators of a need for something, whether it's change, food, or connection. What is it in particular about anger that is so unwieldy?

Emotions and Anger

Our human experience has some similarities to the animal kingdom. We share one part of our three-part brain with the reptiles and then two parts with our fellow mammals. Our reptilian brain doesn't experience emotions per se but has a deep reactivity to direct stimulation and simple responses to those stimuli. For instance, the sun hits my back, so I go under the shade of a rock—a fight or flight response. The limbic system, where the emotions are centered, is an evolutionary design improvement to help get needs met more dynamically. Here we see attachment behaviors like love and bonding, particularly between young ones and caregivers. This fosters connection and reproduction as well as some extra fuel for fight or flight to be exercised. As humans, we have another part of the brain that enables us to have something called executive function to manage these emotions and allows us to assess outcomes and make meaning from experiences and memories. Emotions, including anger, are a vital aspect of the experience of being human. Anger alerts us to unmet needs, which helps us set boundaries and make healthier connections with people. It helps us be creative, have a heart, actively offer compassion, and produce change when change is needed. So why do we have to manage that which is vital and normal?

The reason is this: When unmanaged, anger has so many destructive qualities. When we are triggered we often literally lose access to our cognitive abilities, and we must find strategies to help reduce or channel this energy so that our human gift of reasoning can kick in and contribute. Notice that nothing in this statement asks us to tamp down the anger, or to make it disappear, or to stuff it far down into our unconscious. We need to manage anger so that we can avoid the consequences of acting it out and we can reap the benefits of understanding and utilizing this powerful energy.

In my anger management groups, I have two kinds of participants: those who need to manage anger because the consequences of acting on anger have led to problems in their lives, and those who repress their anger and whose inability to express the emotion in healthy ways has also led to problems in their lives. In my years of running what I would call "mixed" anger management groups–groups that contain both kinds of participants–I have seen some patterns. Those patterns actually informed my decision to have my anger management groups mixed in this way. One environment where I do anger management work is in an addiction treatment setting. What seems clear, at least in that particular group setting, is that one purpose of addictive thoughts and behaviors is to either make anger go away or to enable anger to come out and have its place in the sun. On one side of the group are those who act out their rage, using substances to reduce inhibitions and to massage the anger into action. On the other side are those who say, "I never get angry" or "I'm not allowed to get angry," and their symptoms of distress manifest in a different way—as anxiety, depression, or other problems. Their addiction is designed to calm the distress caused by those symptoms and to make sure that the anger doesn't rise to consciousness and action.

These two types of people seem like opposites, but in fact they are more akin to two sides of a coin. The problem is not anger per se but their relationship to anger. Addictions in this case are used to maintain a distance from anger, to make it so that they are not mindful of their anger. It is a completely understandable strategy when manifesting in either direction—expression or lack of expression. However, the side effects and potential consequences are too great for it to be sustainable. If you do not identify as someone with addictions, utilize this example to see where you fall in the continuum. If you have picked up this book, you are considering the impact of anger on your well-being and looking to see where you can make adjustments and use some tools to improve the quality of your life. Is your difficulty skewed toward an inability to have sufficient agency over your anger response? Or are you leaning more toward the fear of anger, generating strategies designed to ignore it, to make it go away?

One way to understand anger is to see it in the context of our other emotions. Robert Plutchik, a 20th-century psychologist, asserted that we have eight core emotions: fear, sadness, joy, surprise, trust, anticipation, disgust, and anger. Of course, we have a great number of variations and manifestations of these core emotions, but they make a great list to begin an initial consideration of how anger fits into the emotional palette. In addition, this fact can help us understand not only that anger has its own place in that palette but that it also has a deep and powerful relationship to all of the other core emotions.

FEAR

Fear drives much of what we do in our daily lives. We can start with the fear of death and work our way backward. Fear is a key element of our survival instinct. Like all the other animals, either consciously or unconsciously we are continually scanning for danger at some level. In modern

times we are less often looking out for predators than for other indica-
tions of threats to our safety. In terms of our reactivity to perceived or
real danger, fear is the great motivator.

Fear biologically generates our fight or flight response. The more
primitive parts of our brain that are dedicated to maintaining safety will
override our reasoning abilities and our other emotions to help us survive. Often the fear is unfounded, but the system doesn't know that. The
freeze response can also be enacted by fear, which can bring on disso-
ciative responses to situations. Because fear generates fight or flight,
we're given a direct hit on this matter of anger: the fight response. One
of our built-in responses to fear is to attempt to set a boundary with our
anger. Fear is guarding against the loss of something, and anger kicks in
to attempt to assure that loss does not occur, whether it's loss of safety,
respect, material things, state of being, or a belief.

SADNESS

For many decades, people across the spectrum have described anger as
a "secondary emotion." My belief is a little different. I believe that anger is
a primary emotion, though it also comes in behind all the other emotions
at one time or another. Sadness is one of the most often cited emotions
for which anger is implicated in either hiding or replacing it. The close
relationship between sadness and anger in Kübler-Ross' five stages of
grief speaks to their interconnection. The denial and bargaining stages of
grief contain elements of suppressed anger, and then the anger and sadness stages express the underlying feelings related to the loss. Sadness
is well documented as a healthy and normal emotion in medical literature, psychology, philosophy, Shakespeare, poetry, pop songs, and beyond.
Anger often can be unexpressed sadness—another sign that suppressing
is not the best strategy, not only with anger but with all emotions.

JOY

Joy allows us to access all the beauty and wonder in life. Love of all kinds,
being in the flow, the home team winning, a delicious meal, friendship,

art and music—all of these and more bring us joy. Much like anger, joy can seem to arise spontaneously, but more often it is triggered into arising from an internal or external cue. Anger's most common secondary arising in relationship to joy is when joy fades or takes a break. One of the core principles of mindfulness practice is that all things, feelings, and sensations are impermanent, and most of us would like joy to be permanent. So when it inevitably exits the scene, anger can arise in response to the loss.

Many longtime mindfulness practitioners tell the story of their first taste of the very deep sense of joy and contentment that comes from the practice, often lasting for hours or days but leaving a trail of anger in its wake. Some of us have difficulty holding on to positive affect states such as joy, and anger can be one of the go-to states when we cannot maintain that positivity, because it gives us power and energy to continue on.

SURPRISE

Surprise can be pleasant or unpleasant. When it is pleasant, any fear that accompanies it is quickly overridden by the joy or other pleasing state that goes with it. When it is unpleasant, anger can come in for the assist either in the moment of surprise or later on. Unpleasant surprises can generate fear, which creates the fight or flight response, which then puts us in danger of anger taking over.

TRUST

Trust is one of those healthy attachment-driven emotions designed to help us get our needs met. Trust enables relationships both shallow and deep to continue and thrive through repeated trustworthy words and actions. Because of the importance of trust building in creating a safe emotional environment, the breaking of trust can be one of the most damaging emotional events in a person's life. A great number of the unhealed traumatic wounds that people suffer in childhood are related to trust bonds that have been dissolved or broken. Anger represents a healthy but difficult to manage response to these kinds of attachment ruptures. Less egregious trust busting from caregivers or others can also produce the anger response, especially if it has been part of a pattern through the person's life, particularly in childhood.

ANTICIPATION

Anticipation is a trigger for pleasure or excitement on the positive side. We can relish the feeling of anticipation of an upcoming vacation; we may be excited about a new opportunity at work; or we may have positive feelings of anticipation on our way to a first date. However, the shadow side of anticipation is anxiety. Sadness that goes way beyond the normal range can turn to depression, and anticipation that goes exponential can become generalized anxiety. Anxiety and anger are so intertwined that when we are tracking our anger, we often need to track our anxiety as well. When I ask participants of my anger management groups to describe their anger, many have a hard time separating it from their anxiety. Anger can be generated by the stress of anxiety, which can be generated from negatively experienced anticipation.

DISGUST

Disgust is one of the easier emotions to connect to anger. When we are repulsed by something, there can be anger embedded in the response and/or anger that follows. If the disgust continues and the anger becomes attached, a more long-term anger response like resentment can kick in.

ANGER

Then there is anger as a primary emotion. A major theme that will recur in this book is anger as the great setter of boundaries. Healthy experiencing and expressing of anger is a normal and vital aspect of setting healthy boundaries. When a personal boundary has been violated, whether physical, mental, emotional, or spiritual, anger steps in to state and also enforce the previously set boundary or the new appropriate boundary.

Without anger and its fierce wisdom, we would not be able to gather the courage to stand up for ourselves when a situation calls for that kind of strength. When people see injustice, whether interpersonal or societal, the anger that comes up is part of what creates the potential for action and then the action itself. Without this energy of anger, there would be no assertiveness, no motivation. This describes the healthy side of anger, perhaps the side with which we have less familiarity. We will land on this subject again as we progress, but for now we must talk about the problem at hand: anger that is being mismanaged.

)))→ Emergency Tip

One of the most fundamental on-the-spot anger management techniques is to ... well, get away from the spot you are on. Any time that's possible, if you can literally walk away long enough to cool down, there is a better chance that you will de-escalate the situation rather than escalate. In that regard, leaving the triggering situation is helpful in and of itself. In addition, the very action of walking, allowing the cortisol and adrenaline to work themselves out, allows your body to calm and the wiser part of your brain to get back online.

WHEN A HEALTHY EMOTION GETS OUT OF CONTROL

Anger is a healthy emotion, but it is quite easy for it to get out of control. First of all, we are beholden to the reality of our biology. Our body is set up for survival first and foremost, and any time the body perceives its safety to be compromised, a sequence of operations is set in motion. In particular, the amygdala and other parts of the brain responsible for alerting the system to engage fight or flight become the driver of our experience. When the amygdala fires in this way, blood flow to the neocortex slows down in order to place more attention and energy on fight or flight. This is a normal and necessary response in a variety of situations.

However, either in the midst of a single event, or as the result of a number of difficulties experienced over time, the amygdala and the fight or flight system can become oversensitive and fully hijack the brain at times. Blood flow to the neocortex can slow to a stop, and the fight reaction may be enacted far beyond what the situation calls for. This is where the danger arises for anger mismanagement and acting out. This is where road rage has us follow a car that cut us off; this is where we start a fight at the gas station when someone takes our pump; this is where we call our dear one a name we would never call them otherwise; this is when we rant at work within earshot of our colleagues. This is where rage or subrage levels of anger can be acted out to the detriment of others or ourselves. This is the anger management dilemma.

What do we do in the moment to keep our anger from overflowing and causing us to do or say things in an unskillful manner? What do we do for the long haul to experience less anger as a bottom line emotion? What do we do to acknowledge and then manage the triggers that get to us most often? How do we deal with the fact that life is filled with daily and sometimes even moment-to-moment conflict, thereby demanding that we have strategies that are helpful to ourselves and others? How can we get our needs met sufficiently so that we spend less of our time angry and more of our time feeling balance or even joy?

⟫⟫→ BASIC ANGER ASSESSMENT

Answer this simple set of True or False questions to begin examining your anger management needs.

1. I have a tendency to pick at others over behavior that upsets me. For example, I am always complaining about what others do or how they react.   TRUE / FALSE

2. I easily blow up when someone says something that I do not agree with or when people disagree with me.   TRUE / FALSE

3. When I am angry, I have problems controlling my emotions and actions, often saying or doing things that I do not really mean.
TRUE / FALSE

4. I often feel guilty after I have been angry with someone.
TRUE / FALSE

5. I can easily become furious if someone teases or jokes with me.
TRUE / FALSE

6. When I am angry, I find it really difficult to discuss a problem in a controlled manner.   TRUE / FALSE

7. I feel a need to be in control all the time. I'm unwilling to let others take the lead.   TRUE / FALSE

8. I explode inside when I am not getting my way.   TRUE / FALSE

9. I feel upset when others make mistakes.   TRUE / FALSE

10. I often become upset while driving, because someone in front of me is driving too slowly.   TRUE / FALSE

11. I have experienced problems in my relationship, at work, or with my friends and family due to my anger.   TRUE / FALSE

12. When someone says even the slightest negative thing about me, I feel like I am about to explode inside.   TRUE / FALSE

13. I have been in trouble with the law due to my anger.   TRUE / FALSE

14. When I am angry I can physically feel it in my body: My heart rate increases, I breathe faster, my body trembles, I sweat, etc. TRUE / FALSE

15. I have used some type of substance (like alcohol, drugs, or medication) to calm me down.   TRUE / FALSE

16. I have physically hurt others or myself while I was angry. TRUE / FALSE

Now count the number of times you selected TRUE.

1 to 4 = Going through this book will help you understand your anger so that you can manage it more skillfully.

5 to 8 = While going through this book will help you understand and manage your anger, it may be helpful to engage others in doing this work, whether through dedicated support groups or a circle of friends working on the book with you.

9 or more = This book will help you understand your anger so that you can manage it, though it may be helpful to engage others in doing this work and to consider professional guidance to deal with any issues that are feeding the anger or working side by side with anger. A dedicated support group or a circle of friends working on the book with you is also recommended.

Each of these describes possible triggers and/or symptoms of mismanaged anger. They do not offer a diagnosis, a scarlet letter, or an excuse for a shame spiral. This is a self-assessment and a starting point. You can come back to this questionnaire as you go through the chapters of this book and see if your responses change as one way of tracking progress.

WHEN TO SEEK HELP

In the world of therapy and treatment, we like to find the lowest level of care for a person. Some people will be able to work with the anger management techniques in this book on their own and get the maximum benefit. That would be the lowest level of care. Some readers will benefit from having friends or family supporting them in this process, whether they are doing the exercises alongside you or just knowing you are in this process and being available for you when you need help along the way. A higher level of care would be getting professional help for your anger management difficulties. If your anger is getting in the way of your functioning at work in a significant way, if you are fighting with loved ones to the point of possible irreparable harm to the relationship, if things are getting physical, or if the anger is causing or being caused by a psychological/emotional difficulty such as depression, anxiety, addiction, or PTSD, then going to a professional will be a critical component of your journey. Working with this book with a professional will help you keep your focus on the anger management aspect of your care and may very well help you with your other diagnoses or difficulties.

Deciding to Change

Even with the most compelling argument in favor of changing your relationship to anger, changing old habits can be incredibly difficult. For some people, change in general feels difficult or even insurmountable. The fear of the unknown keeps one from taking steps, positive or otherwise. Another barrier to making changes is that the thinking or behaviors in question may have been "working" up until now. Perhaps anger has brought you gifts in life, like your surviving through difficulties, or even positive consequences on the job or in a relationship. In the world of trauma, addiction, and anger management, we clinicians often talk about how maladaptive responses and strategies are most often adaptive at first. I zone out from a traumatic event in order to get through it. I use substances to keep my depression or anxiety at bay.

I stay angry to have some feeling of power or agency in my life. These are hard habits and thought patterns to change when they have been keeping me alive and feeling sane.

That being said, you have made quite the courageous move in opening the pages of this book and making a commitment to yourself to make such a change. Regardless of your particular obstacles, it takes a great deal of courage, motivation, action, faith, and strength to walk through the valley of one's own anger history and coping styles and, with fresh eyes, make new connections and decisions about how to deal with anger. If mindfulness has been unfamiliar to you until now, then that is an extra layer of courage and faith that you are harnessing—the willingness to try something that might seem counterintuitive at this moment. I admire your courage.

THE COST OF ANGER

The cost of anger is incredibly high and can be measured in a number of ways. If left unattended, untreated, or mismanaged, anger can bring more and more negative consequences over time. If you find yourself getting physical with your anger, this response only gets reinforced over time, and the obvious terrible physical harm that can result from an unintended outburst of anger can change lives forever. The emotional harm that comes from unrelenting anger in a relationship can do horrendous damage to both individuals—the perpetrator of the anger and the victim—as well as the invisible third party: the relationship itself.

Unbridled anger tends to keep people from being able to access spiritual resources that they would otherwise utilize to improve their quality of life. From a biological perspective, ongoing anger problems leave a person with an ongoing flow of stress hormones and the physical, mental, and emotional stress that goes with that. We know now that stress in general is implicated in everything from having less energy to sleep problems to a variety of illnesses and conditions including cancer. If anger is not managed well, then the overall level of stress may remain elevated, and these medical and psychological consequences may arise.

We could also put a dollar amount on the loss, whether it's lost productivity, lost jobs, loss of reputation resulting in lower income, loss of a marriage resulting in legal costs, therapy for any children involved in a divorce—the list goes on.

COMMITTING TO CHANGE

Even weighing these possible consequences against the possible gains to be had through change, you may still have some hesitation. It is completely natural and utterly understandable. Making a commitment can be hard. So here is some of the language of mindfulness practice to help you along.

In the long-standing traditional teachings of mindfulness, a key to successful mindfulness practice includes integrating ethical living and wisdom with the practice of meditation. The two factors of wisdom that are outlined are wise understanding and the setting of wise intention. The reason wise understanding comes first among all the factors is that one needs just enough understanding to know that trying new things—like the path outlined in this book—would be a good idea. So, you have already achieved wise understanding by reading to this point.

Now, instead of a steadfast commitment that might be too easy to break, leaving you no longer motivated because of a feeling of failure, let us set an intention to move ahead with the next pages of this book. One aspect of wise understanding is knowing that we are setting and resetting intention in every moment, with every decision and action large and small. So below, you may sign your intention to move ahead and commit only to resetting your intention as necessary along the way.

I, _____ , am setting my intention to continue reading and working in this book. I also set the intention to reset my intention as necessary, knowing that faltering is not failure and that my energy can be renewed with new intention at any time.

Signed, _____

Mindfulness for Anger

Now that we understand a little more about anger in general and have set our intention, what about mindfulness? What is mindfulness, and what makes it a skill for anger management? Can it be learned and applied? Is it like going to the gym, or do I memorize some techniques and flip a switch?

I am going to answer these questions first by introducing you to the core mindfulness-based anger exercise that I have used for over 25 years now to help people begin their journey with anger—one that will continue to assist you as you move along in this book and then for a lifetime if you choose.

THE MINDFULNESS OF ANGER SCALE

A scale from 0 to 10 is used in many scenarios, including in the medical world, so that professionals can get a sense of where a patient is regarding pain, anxiety, or other difficulties. Many years ago, I began to use an Anger Check-in 0 to 10 scale in order to help people monitor their levels of anger **in this very moment**. We'll use this scale throughout the book as a way for you to begin making a habit of checking in with yourself. It is from this scale that we are able to then measure formally or informally a whole host of anger-related information, enabling us to tailor strategies and skills to that particular person and set of circumstances.

Check in with yourself for a moment. You may close your eyes if you like. Here is my question for you:

On a scale of 0 to 10, what is your level of anger in this moment?

Zero and 10 are the only absolutes on the scale that are pretty much the same for everyone. Zero is very rare, and let me describe it: Imagine someone comes up to you and calls you a number of expletives, says they hate you, and then spits in your face. Your response to all this at a true 0 is "namaste" or the equivalent.

And we are talking a true namaste, not bowing with prayer hands as you imagine stabbing the person while the *Curse of Chucky* soundtrack plays in your mind. Like I said, a 0 is very, very rare.

Now, 10 is as if you were unable to control yourself at all. You throw this book down on the ground, head for the nearest unopened window, jump through it, roll around in the broken glass for a bit, and then head out into the street, where you haul off and punch the first vehicle you see. This is a 10 because a person at a 10 can be in an actual blackout, with or without the addition of mind-altering substances. The blood flow to the neocortex stops, the hippocampus shuts down, no new memories are being created in the moment, and the very poor decisions of jumping through unopened windows and punching cars are enacted. Just like 0, 10 is also very rare.

Zero and 10 are pretty much the same for all people. From 0.1 to 9.9 is different for everyone. One person's 4 is another person's 6. This is where the scale becomes personal, and it becomes potentially changeable over time. So, on this next line, go ahead and take your first opportunity to determine where you are on the scale **in this moment**.

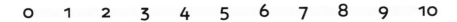

Welcome to your mindfulness-based anger management journey. In traditional mindfulness teachings, it is said that once you become mindful of the fact that you are in a state of anger, you are no longer inside the anger state but rather in a state of mindfulness of the anger state. This is just enough mindfulness to begin practicing.

The problem with unchecked anger is that one angry thought or sensation locks into another and into another and so on until we are far along on a journey called "monkey mind." The story gets bigger and more entrenched, and the anger level goes up. By doing this exercise, we are immediately able to enlist mindfulness as our aid and have the opportunity to go further into mindfulness rather than further into the anger. Also, probably the biggest obstacle to anger management is a lack of mindfulness of our triggers and of the arrival of our anger. The sooner we are able to intervene on a trigger or acknowledge our being angry, the greater chance we have to manage it. So, to begin our path of seeing if we can deepen the mindfulness rather than the anger, on the lines below, write a sentence or two exploring why you are right now at the number you checked off on the scale above.

_____

_____

_____

You are now officially practicing mindfulness. Now you know that mindfulness is not all sitting in lotus position on the beach in your best yoga clothes. Mindfulness is a practical skill set that can be learned and applied in a variety of situations. And the good news is that even the ancient version of mindfulness practice was in part designed specifically for anger management, an increase in a feeling of kindness toward self and others, and overall well-being.

So, you are about to commence a journey that is time tested through the millennia, evidence-based according to modern-day science, and infinitely practical and applicable to day-to-day life—and extraordinarily accessible to everyone. All that is required is the intention coupled with a human body and mind to work with. As of this moment, you have all the components.

In the following chapter, let's look a little more closely at anger and begin to apply mindfulness to our own unique anger management scenarios.

CHAPTER 2

Why Am I Angry?

This chapter deepens our exploration of what our anger is and what is beneath our anger. An important aspect of this particular exploration is looking at the unmet needs triggering the anger. We'll try to answer this question together: What are we really saying when we're angry?

A Deeper Look at Anger

Anger for the most part does not happen in a vacuum. There is some kind of internal or external trigger that brings on the physical, emotional, and psychological responses. It can be helpful to list and analyze anger triggers, such as unmet needs, insecurity, past hurts, unprocessed trauma, present danger, and historical relationships.

Let's look at an example of anger difficulties in one family. Joseph is a successful accountant who lives with his wife and two teenage children. He does not struggle with anger management problems at work, where he is well respected, and his colleagues would agree. At home, however, his temper flares quickly with his wife, Samantha, but only around one subject: their parenting styles. Samantha prefers to discipline the kids with harsh words and quick consequences, and Joseph prefers a softer approach, the same one he uses at work. When he and Samantha disagree on how to handle too much screen time for the children, it turns into scream time for Joseph. Now anger is coming out through Samantha toward the children and from Joseph toward Samantha. Everyone in the house is angry.

UNMET NEEDS

What is causing the cycle of anger in this home? The best way to analyze this situation is to look at the unmet needs throughout the household. The children are angry because their perceived need for screen time is not being met, and they are experiencing harsh language from their mother, which leaves their needs for peace and respect unmet. Samantha learned her style of discipline from her parents and feels disrespected by Joseph's alternative parenting style. The anger she receives from him leaves her with unmet emotional and safety needs. And, finally, Joseph's needs for peace in the home and to parent the way he sees fit are not being met.

INSECURITIES

There are many triggers related to insecurity, which can lead to low self-esteem. It can be related to body image, intelligence, competence at work or school, or lack of athletic or artistic ability. All of this may be real or perceived. There can be emotional insecurity in a relationship where the trust factor is weak or there is a system of shutting down when faced with intimacy, resulting in loneliness or distance. Financial insecurity also commonly leads to anger problems. So many marriages and other romantic relationships are decimated by anger management difficulties that manifest out of financial strain.

In our example above, Joseph has insecurity about his ability as a parent, since his system that gives him such positive feedback at work does not succeed at home. Samantha feels insecurity because she believes her parenting style is right; she holds a deep belief that her parents were right about most if not all things, and this belief makes her rigid, controlling, and insecure all at once. And the kids feel insecure because they live in constant fear of their parents getting angry to the point of splitting up.

PAST HURTS

In 12-step recovery programs there are many slogans. Some are somewhat official while others pop up in local recovery cultures. One popular slogan I learned on the East Coast during my recovery is "If it's hysterical, it's historical." So often when people are yelling or acting out their anger in some way, they are not yelling so much at the person in front of them as they are at a parent they are still angry with or a younger version of the person in front of them. Looking at past hurts in this context of anger management is so important because we do not want to just gloss over those past hurts; we need to turn toward them with mindfulness in order to have the ability to make new decisions about our actions and relationships in the present. We need to find ways to validate our experience but also find our way to some level of forgiveness in order to move on. Until we have that forgiveness, we may be doomed to repeat anger behaviors again and again when faced with something that reminds us of the past hurt, even if it's below the level of consciousness.

UNPROCESSED TRAUMAS

We now have a much better understanding of the role of unprocessed traumas in the anger cycle. As an EMDR therapist and trainer, I have seen how people develop symptoms of anger mismanagement whether they have diagnosable PTSD, unprocessed trauma below the PTSD threshold, or even unprocessed memories that the person would describe simply as adverse life events. Regardless, if the material from the trauma gets stuck in the amygdala or another primitive part of the brain, or in the body, those sensations, affects, and noncognitive aspects of the memory are now potential triggers for present-time anger. This is because those parts of the brain have no sense of time as we know it in our conscious lives, so when the trigger gets tickled, whatever happened in the past is happening again **now**.

So, for instance, when a combat veteran hears a loud sound and dives under a desk for cover, she is not thinking, *It's 2018, and I am home, and that's just a loud sound, but I'd better duck for cover anyway.* She's thinking, feeling, and believing in that moment that she is back in the original traumatic situation. This explains why amygdala hijacking happens. The amygdala is simply responding to the threat that has been coded into it. That memory was not adaptively processed through to the neocortex, which can say, "Yes, that happened, it was awful, but it's not happening now." Part of every anger management program needs to be addressing this issue of unprocessed trauma in some form or fashion. You will have exercises throughout this book that address it, but if your trauma history is profound, seeking extra support from a professional is highly recommended.

HISTORICAL RELATIONSHIPS

How is this category different from some of the above? Even fairly well-adjusted relationships can generate anger. Conflict is a part of life, so when people spend a great deal of their lives together as friends or family, conflict will come up. And sometimes it doesn't take a huge degree of dysfunction for people within a relationship to develop poor communication when it comes to anger, especially if they have different anger styles and histories. Another informal slogan in recovery circles: "Your family knows how to push your buttons because they installed them." We need to have mindfulness of the power of our historical relationships to develop a full-bodied anger management protocol for ourselves.

PRESENT DANGER

Of course, not all anger is based on history. Sometimes present danger unrelated to any history can bring up the anger response. In this case, having worked on all the historical anger pays off. If the fight or flight response has only the present danger to lock into, it will be easier to go through the entire sequence of the flooding of cortisol and adrenaline to put the body into action. It will take about an hour for all the hormonal and neurochemical changes to fade away and exit. The neocortex will then be able to engage again, creating meaning and a long-term memory out of the incident.

ANGER AS AVOIDANCE

Another way that anger manifests is through avoidance. Remember the mixed anger management groups? There are the people who act on their anger and mix it up with the people in their lives, and then there are those who avoid people and situations through a number of different maladaptive strategies. These include, but are not limited to, procrastination; denying or avoiding reality; worrying; avoiding feelings, relationships, or confrontation; experiencing bodily symptoms; perfectionism; distraction; substitutes (drug and alcohol use and other addictive behaviors); lying; withdrawal; seeking to live a busy life; sarcasm; habits (seeking familiarity); turning down opportunities; not taking things seriously; avoiding decisions; analyzing; judging; criticizing; and excessive preoccupation with an event, symptom, past failure, or others' failures to meet our expectations.

If this list seems extensive, that's because it represents all the nuanced ways that different people will avoid this difficult emotion. In the end, of course, the anger manifests in one of these ways or some other way. With many of these, the primary form of anger becomes anger at self because of the consequences of many of these maladaptive coping mechanisms. Stress continues to plague the procrastinator and the worrier, addictions develop, relationships suffer under the burden of passive-aggressive sarcasm, distractions become the norm rather than the temporary escape, and loneliness sets in with the avoidance of people and situations.

As noted earlier, avoidance is just another response to anger and does not require a different anger management tool kit. Of course, the person who manifests on the acting out side of the continuum needs to find ways to dial down the anger while the person who is avoidant will need to learn how to feel their anger in order to access it and work with it in new ways. However, in the end, both of these people will be working their way toward the middle using similar mindfulness practices to get there.

For many years, the classic suggestion for emergency anger management was to count to 10. This definitely works for some people, but notice if you need something slightly different. Some people can count to 10 internally and have their anger level reduce by the count of 4 or 5 while others find themselves escalating and internally shouting the numbers. Look into other options if this is true for you. Perhaps you want to take three deep breaths because you are able to feel the oxygen filling your lungs, slowing down the blood pressure and the breathing rate. Or maybe you can feel your feet grounded into the floor, focusing keenly on the sensation. Or you can combine two or all three of these into an emergency strategy.

ANGER TYPES

There are a number of categories that psychologists and others have found to describe different anger types and styles. For our purposes, let's keep it simple and go with the six major categories: explosive anger, self-abusive anger, avoidance, sarcasm, passive-aggressive anger, and ongoing irritation.

ANGER TYPES AND THEIR TRAITS

Explosive anger is what we are most familiar with when we talk about anger. It is when a person acts out. It can be a steady stream of explosive behavior and verbiage, or it can come in binges. It can be verbal, physical, or a combination. Often, there is a Jekyll and Hyde aspect to the explosive anger person. When they are not in their anger, they are often charming and disarming.

Self-abusive anger often manifests in depression and anxiety. As opposed to acting out, the person is acting in. There is fear or shame attached to the idea of acting the anger out, but it has nowhere else to go, so the self-abusive anger person will turn it all inward. It may manifest in explosive ways toward the self, like self-harm, or in quiet rage that has been transmuted into other problems like depression.

Avoidance people will do everything in their power to stay out of conflict. They may have a reputation as a peacemaker or as a really "nice" person. By not allowing themselves to have their anger, they often will manifest symptoms similar to the self-abusive types.

Sarcasm will go a long way if you want to have a special on Comedy Central, but in real life it becomes a painful way to be in relationship with others. The Greek derivation of the word means "to tear flesh." I think that sums up the anger aspect of sarcasm quite nicely.

Passive-aggressive is a term that is thrown around a lot, maybe because there are many passive-aggressive people in the world. It's when anger comes out sideways, through small actions and subtle words that don't express directly the anger that is felt, but the message gets across over time.

Ongoing irritation is a strategy used by people who refuse to take on the admonition not to sweat the small stuff. They sweat all of the stuff. And like the passive-aggressive, it's not really about the small stuff; it's the bigger stuff underneath.

Identifying Your Anger Triggers

Anger triggers are not cookie-cutter. One person's disaster is another person's "nothing to see here, folks." You can use the following list as a thumbnail of some of the ways that people find themselves taken over by anger, thrown into a cycle of acting out or acting in.

Injustice: Many people see injustice all around them. There are the larger societal issues but also perceived slights directed either at themselves or at a friend or family member.

Disrespect: When I was working as a negotiation specialist at a high school, disrespect was the term most often used to describe a triggering event. This tends to carry over into adult life as well, since respect is a fundamental need.

Violation of your personal space: This can range from the worst of violations, such as physical abuse, all the way down to simply feeling crowded by other people.

Abusive language/insults: In some cultures or situations, abusive language is commonplace, and people tend to let it go. However, if the abusive language locks in to past abuse, anger will arise.

Labeling, shaming, blaming: This covers societal territory in the form of prejudice, discrimination, and stereotyping as well as inter-personal territory, which can include historical relationships or single-event conflicts.

Physical threats: Any threat to one's physical safety is going to trigger the fight or flight response. It depends on the anger management level of the people involved, but once we are in this territory, intervention becomes more difficult.

Misinformation: Anger can kick in due to misinformation across the spectrum, whether it's a faulty news source on your social media feed or someone giving incorrect directions to a party. Depending on your anger management readiness, anything on this continuum could start the anger cycle.

Lying: Often people find themselves lying as a way of avoiding conflict, thus setting up a possible anger-producing event in the future. And those people who are lied to and discover the lie will feel violated.

Relationship disputes: This needs almost no explanation. Romantic relationships, marriages, dating relationships ... they were built for anger management training. And the amygdala is on high alert, cognitive abilities be damned.

Constant disappointment: Most people have the capacity to deal with a disappointment here and there, but when life seems like an endless parade of disappointments, the anger management muscle is challenged.

Lack of control: There is very little that is under our control at any time. Whether the feeling of lack of control is undeniable, like weather patterns or traffic, or deniable, like getting a speeding ticket, this feeling can trigger the anger response.

Particular individuals: You know that person? You know the one. They are just so ... annoying. The way they crack their gum. The way they don't like *The Sopranos*. The way they chew with their mouth open sometimes, mouth closed others—you can't even depend on them to be consistent! Sometimes someone pushes some sort of button(s), and you are powerless over your anger.

➤➤➤ EXERCISE: TRIGGERS, PART 1

For your first exercise regarding your unique triggers, think back on the last week and make a list of the top 10 things that caused you to express anger in an unhealthy way. You can use the above list of triggers and the Basic Anger Assessment (on page 11) we did earlier to help you. Remember, this too is a mindfulness exercise. Give yourself the space and time, close your eyes (or leave them open if you prefer) while you think, and then on the lines below write down your most recent anger triggers. What we are treating with this book is the way anger is manifesting in your life today. This list may change before we finish our work together and is sure to change as you continue your work beyond this book.

Maslow's hierarchy of needs provides a solid framework for looking at the needs that are contained within many of our most common triggers. When you think of these needs not being met, especially those that are most closely tied to survival, you are able to see the value of anger, the normalcy of anger, and the role of anger in setting boundaries and finding ways to get needs met.

Physiological: These needs are the most basic related to a person's survival. They consist of breathing, food, water, sleep, excretion, sex, clothing, and shelter. Without most of these things, a body cannot physically function. Think of any time you have been hungry. Think of times when you could not get to a bathroom. Think of how quick you are to anger when you haven't slept versus when you've had a good night's sleep. Think of when you may have been too cold or too hot or without a place to stay. Think of times when you have not had physical intimacy with anyone and it was not your preference. All of these can trigger anger.

Safety: A person's safety needs can relate to several factors in their life, such as health, finances, physical security, and emotional security. They say that all you have is your health. When health is compromised, we may feel unsafe. When there's not enough money around, whether real or perceived, the stress and worry can cause anger. Perhaps your physical and emotional security have been compromised, whether by a family member, a friend, or a stranger. Anger steps in to try to get those needs met.

Love/Belonging: These are social needs, often seen as the need to belong, whether it's in the category of friendship, intimacy, or family. Similar to physiological needs and safety, being deprived of love and belonging can be severely compromising. Any event or situation that either stops us from belonging or separates us from those we love can bring on the highest degree of anger.

Esteem: Each person has a need to feel respected and have self-esteem. This is also related to issues of having a sense of accomplishment or achievement. At this point we are further away from the bottom-line survival instinct, but we are still in the human dimension of needs. Not having these needs met can also bring about an anger jag.

Self-actualization: This describes a person's need to achieve what they believe they are meant to achieve; to meet this need is to reach their potential. This need is never truly fully met, but rather it evolves as they develop psychologically, emotionally, and spiritually. Often these higher levels of development come with the internal resources and the resilience to not fall into the anger trap, but as with all the others, boundaries are boundaries.

COMMON TRIGGERS	ASSOCIATED EMOTIONAL NEEDS
Injustice	Justice, fairness, kindness
Disrespect	Respect
Violation of personal space	Feelings of safety and autonomy
Abusive language/insults	Respect, self-esteem, kindness
Labeling, shaming, blaming	Respect, esteem, being seen as an individual
Physical threats	Safety
Misinformation	To be clear of confusion
Lying	Trust
Relationship disputes	Trust, intimacy
Constant disappointment	Achievement
Lack of control	Control and agency
Particular individuals	For others to act a certain way

Identifying Reasonable versus Unreasonable Expectations

One of the most famous and oft quoted chapters in the 12-step literature revolves around acceptance. In that chapter, entitled "Acceptance is the Answer," the author writes, "The level of my serenity is inversely proportional to the level of my expectations." When we set our expectations too high for ourselves, for our loved ones, for the world, for all of life's moments, we will almost always be disappointed.

Mindfulness practice, in many ways, is designed to regulate our expectations. As a Zen teacher said to me many years ago, "For every thousand things you do, three will go your way." Now, this is not a hardhearted exercise that asks us to lower our expectations to a flat line or a completely dull life but rather a weeding out of toxic expectations that go counter to reality and that trigger anger. Following is a list of some unreasonable expectations or "shoulds," and below each one is the more reasonable expectation that might replace it. Dealing with these "shoulds" is an anger management super tool.

➤➤➤ REASONABLE VERSUS UNREASONABLE EXPECTATIONS OR "SHOULDS"

1. I should do well and get the approval of everybody who matters to me, or I will be a worthless person.

   I am worthy and worthwhile just as I am.

2. Other people should treat me kindly and fairly, or else they are bad.

   Everyone has some bad and some good in them.

3. I should have an easy, enjoyable life, or I cannot enjoy living at all.

   Life has its challenges, and they make it more interesting.

4. All the people who matter to me should love me and approve of me, or it will be awful.

   It is not so black and white; I can take in the love and approval that is available, and I can give love, too.

5. I should be a high achiever, or I will be worthless.

   I am worthy and worthwhile simply by being a human being.

6. Nobody should ever behave badly, and if they do I should condemn them.

   I can dislike the actions of a person and set boundaries without condemning the person.

7. I shouldn't be frustrated in getting what I want, and if I am it will be terrible.

   Life is a series of disappointments and victories, and I will go with the flow.

8. When things are tough and I am under pressure, I should be miserable, and there is nothing I can do about this.

   I can find the resilience and the strength to deal with pressure situations with equanimity.

9. When faced with the possibility of something frightening or dangerous happening to me, I should obsess about it and make frantic efforts to avoid it.

   If I lean in to the difficulties, I will stay in mindfulness and be able to think clearly.

10. I should be able to avoid my responsibilities and not deal with life's difficulties and still be fulfilled.

    Avoidance is not a strategy; it is only postponing the inevitable conflict to resolve.

11. My past is the most important part of my life, and it should keep on dictating how I feel and what I do.

    My past is filled with lessons and blessings, and I can use it to make the present and future great.

12. Everybody and everything should be better than they are, and if they're not, it's awful.

    I can allow everyone to have their own process.

13. I should be as happy as possible by doing as little as I can and by just enjoying myself.

    The flow of life has ups and downs. It's best if I go ahead and ride the roller coaster. It is where I will find the fun.

When My "Shoulds" Are Broken

One of the great producers of anger is rigidity born of a long list of "shoulds." Whether it was society that told me it was so, or my family, or the institutions that brought me up, or even if I made it up all by myself, shoulds are built from fear; fear results in rigidity; rigidity builds unreasonable expectations and disappointment; and disappointment produces anger. Lack of mindfulness has led us down blind pathways of thought, emotion, and sensation. We then crash into walls of unreasonable expectations.

"Right now it's like this" is a favorite teaching of modern mindfulness teachers, and it can go a long way in reducing the intensity of these "shoulds." There is no way that things *should* be... they simply are. This is a belief and a skill that we will be building together throughout this book.

⟫⟫→ LOOKING UNDERNEATH THE HOOD OF "SHOULDS"

Let's take an even closer look at "shoulds." As I mentioned earlier, anger is trying to communicate something, but what? Below is the list of "shoulds" from earlier, and below each one is a possible underlying hurt beneath the expectation. Can you relate to any?

1. I should do well and get the approval of everybody who matters to me, or I will be a worthless person.

   I'm afraid no one will ever think I'm good enough.

2. Other people should treat me kindly and fairly, or else they are bad.

   I'm afraid people will see me as unkind.

3. I should have an easy, enjoyable life, or I cannot enjoy living at all.

   I am afraid I will fail if I try difficult things.

4. All the people who matter to me should love me and approve of me, or it will be awful.

   I am afraid of being alone.

5. I should be a high achiever, or I will be worthless.

   I am afraid I am unlovable as I am.

6. Nobody should ever behave badly, and if they do I should condemn them.

   I am afraid of being judged.

7. I shouldn't be frustrated about getting what I want, and if I am it will be terrible.

   I have to be a success to be loved.

8. When things are tough and I am under pressure, I should be miserable, and there is nothing I can do about this.

   I am not allowed to be happy.

9. When faced with the possibility of something frightening or dangerous happening to me, I should obsess about it and make frantic efforts to avoid it.

   Reality is scary, and I can't let you know I feel that way.

10. I should be able to avoid my responsibilities and not deal with life's difficulties and still be fulfilled.

    I'm afraid you will see me as weak and incapable.

11. My past is the most important part of my life, and it should keep on dictating how I feel and what I do.

    I have no identity without my story.

12. Everybody and everything should be better than they are, and if they're not, it's awful.

    I am not good enough, and you are going to find that out.

13. I should be as happy as possible by doing as little as I can and by just enjoying myself.

    The flow of life has ups and downs. It's best if I go ahead and ride the roller coaster. It is where I will find the fun.

⇉➤ EXERCISE: TRIGGERS, PART 2

Write down some personal triggers below. Next to each one write a possible need, a realistic expectation you could replace it with, and an underlying hurt beneath the hood of the trigger. Here's an example to get you started:

TRIGGER	POSSIBLE NEED	REALISTIC EXPECTATION	UNDERLYING HURT
Clerk at the store didn't help me with my questions.	To be treated kindly and fairly	Everyone has some bad and some good in them.	My dad would never listen to me when I was a kid.

»»→ TRIGGERING EVENTS MONITOR

Your first two trigger exercises have laid the foundation for this weekly exercise to track your most recent triggers. Below is a chart for you to mark any triggering events that occurred over the last week and track how you were feeling and what you were thinking during the event. We will repeat

DATE / TIME	TRIGGER	TRIGGER INTENSITY: 0–10
3pm February 9	Guy cut me off on the freeway.	7

this exercise throughout the book to build awareness of your anger, reactions, and responses and to track your growth and progress. Here's an example to get you started:

THOUGHTS	ACTIONS	BODY SENSATIONS
That guy is an idiot and shouldn't have a license.	Gave him the finger.	Angry then fearful of retribution. Spacey; body was hot and flush.

Final Thoughts

At this point we have a sense of what anger is, how it manifests, what triggers it, and how mindfulness might help us manage it. Placing mindfulness upon our triggers, our anger styles, and our daily anger levels brings us to the place where we can deepen and broaden our anger management tool kit. In the next part of our journey, we will make mindfulness a way of life that reduces anger and increases well-being.

PART TWO

SKILLS FOR OVERCOMING ANGER AND MANAGING POWERFUL EMOTIONS

What if you could intervene on anger and actually take back its power over you through awareness? How might you harness and channel this energy to your own benefit? In this section we'll learn concepts and skills to help you do exactly that.

CHAPTER 3

You Are Not Your Anger

When we're in anger, we're fused with it; we think it's who we are. There is no separation. But you are not your anger. You are simply experiencing a dysfunctional response pattern to perceived threats. The more we practice not being anger, the more we can respond to life's challenges skillfully and with kindness. This chapter will show you how to detach and understand that you are not your anger.

In chapter 2 you began to track your anger on a scale of 0 to 10, noticing the subtle variations in the level of your anger from day to day, hour to hour, moment to moment. This exercise and much of what we will learn in this chapter comes down to one important concept and skill: awareness.

⟫⟩→ ANGER CHECK-IN

Quickly spot check yourself to see where your anger is right now in this moment on a scale of 0 to 10. Why do you think you are at your current number? Notice if you have found yourself changing since the beginning of the book and if you have a clearer picture of what your number is on a regular basis. Mark your number on the chart, and use the lines below it to write a few thoughts as to why you are at that number.

0   1   2   3   4   5   6   7   8   9   10

_____

_____

_____

_____

_____

_____

_____

_____

_____

_____

_____

_____

_____

_____

_____

_____

_____

_____

Anger and Awareness

The power of simple awareness has been explored in wisdom traditions throughout the millennia and in modern times has become an important object of meditation in a multitude of arenas, both personal and professional. We have been forced to look deeply at the fragile state of our awareness because of the pace of modern life. The introduction of devices into our moment-to-moment experience has stretched our ability to maintain awareness to its furthest limits. The information of all kinds, including highly emotional information, that we are bombarded with daily leaves us stressed and vulnerable. If there is any good news we can cull from all this, it is that we have been forced to acknowledge, both as individuals and as a collective, that finding ways to cultivate awareness is now nonnegotiable. It is critical for our emotional, psychological, spiritual, and societal health. This is not limited to our work with our anger, but it is most obvious here.

The English-language word *mindfulness* entered the lexicon in 1881 and is a translation of a Sanskrit word meaning "awareness"–more specifically, "coming back to awareness." By this definition, awareness is a skill we can cultivate, not a passive engagement. What is it that takes us away from awareness? There are a number of mental and emotional factors involved–and anger is a major player. Since what we experience as anger is driven by the more primitive survival-oriented parts of the brain–and the parts of the brain that can maintain awareness of states of mind and our general surroundings can go offline during that fight or flight process–it makes sense that anger leads to a lack of awareness. So, our goal in this book and in our lives becomes finding a way to come back to awareness. This is a task that has different manifestations in our short-term and long-term interventions on our anger.

What would it look like to be mindful of anger? The answer lies in the truth about our bodies and minds. Our emotional brain and our highly reactive lizard brain don't really want to hear what the rational mind has to say. And when we get activated enough, blood flow to the rational part of the brain literally slows down or even stops. At that point, not only do we have no agency over our thoughts and actions in the moment, but we may not maintain a coherent memory of the event. This leaves the anger-inducing event in place to both continue to bother us on its own and also exacerbate any future events and reactions that bear some resemblance. This cycle can produce distorted beliefs.

Being mindful of anger is a two-step process. We need to become mindful of how the angry body works so that we can place awareness on it and work with it skillfully. And then we can work on the distorted effects on the rational mind.

⫸⟶ Emergency Tip

Sometimes we just have to use the Who Wants to Be a Millionaire? strategy to manage our anger on the fly: phone a friend. There is an important caveat here. Going to a friend to vent is a useful tool, but not if that friend is someone who specializes in helping you escalate conflicts and fan the flames of your anger. Many of us have different friend groups for different aspects of our lives. There are the friends you go to for easygoing fun and those you go to for the deeper issues of life. Having friends that you can go to who are interested in helping you de-stress and decompress from an angry state of mind is invaluable. The right person can provide a state of relational mindfulness, and working together can help you return to embodied awareness.

FRUSTRATION TOLERANCE

There is another very good reason why awareness gets beaten down by anger. Anger is one of those emotions that is unpleasant and difficult. In fact, a majority of our difficulties and potential diagnoses are the results of an inability to sit with and get through our difficult states of mind. Here are some scenarios that fit this description: You are in a hotel room with your family; there's only one television and one remote—and four different people requesting four different shows. You are in traffic, on your way to a job interview, and you know you are going to be late, ruining the chance to make a good first impression. You find someone you believe is the love of your life, and they give you the "it's not you, it's me" speech.

Whether it's the remote, possible financial insecurity, or frustration of the highest order in your love life, these are potential creators of difficult emotions. These emotions are natural, and often the content of the triggers makes the emotions justifiable. What we might lack is the ability to tolerate these strong emotions in such a way that allows us to understand their energy, feel them, and then let them go.

The ancient mindfulness teachings say that we are absolutely not able to avoid the pain of life, but we can address the extra layer of suffering we place on top of it. It is not the pain of not watching my show that is problematic as much as my opinion about losing that battle with my family members, and then any resistance to the unpleasantness of that loss. It is not the lateness that is killing me but rather my focus on it being the arbiter of everything about my first impression and not something easily explained to the interviewer. And it is not the agony of loss of love as much as it might be about historical beliefs about myself being unconsciously validated, leaving me in a compromised state of fight or flight directed at the person who left me, or at myself.

These strong emotions, including anger, are part of life, and it is in my best interest to learn how to live with them. As human beings we have some wonderful assets in this area. We can think things through. We can make decisions, including decisions about where to place our focus. We can make meaning out of things. We can learn about the nature of reality and our lives on a deep level from our experiences, positive and negative, pleasant or unpleasant. The only way we can tap into these assets, however, is if we cultivate them. We need to take an active role in building our awareness of our feeling states so we can then utilize the rest of our brain to take care of ourselves while going through these feeling states.

This ability is called frustration tolerance, also known as distress tolerance. *Frustration* is one of the synonyms for anger, a bridge to deeper anger states and the acting out of anger. *Distress* can describe any type of stress or distress, any unpleasant sensation, emotion, or cognition, or any strong feeling that can lead to acting out, including acting out in anger. Mindfulness practices are some of the greatest tools we have at our disposal to increase our ability to deal with distress and frustration.

➤➤➤ PRACTICE: RAIN

First described in the 1990s by mindfulness teacher Michele McDonald, the acronym RAIN stands for recognize, allow, investigate, and nurture. Here is a description of RAIN that you can use as an exercise, applying it to whatever you are finding difficult at the moment.

Recognize: The very first step in coming into awareness or back to awareness is to recognize what is happening. A fundamental tool in the mindfulness tool kit is the ability to label an experience in order to start the process of separating ourselves from it. For instance, I might recognize a hot sensation in my throat from anger bubbling. Find the label that will help you see the sensation or emotion or cognition for what it is: a temporary situation that is going to pass and that need not get connected with further sensations, emotions, and cognitions. The moment I recognize the heat in my throat, or the emotion of anger, or the thought *I am so angry*, we can work with it. Notice right now if there is something in your experience that is unpleasant, and see if you can label it in a general way.

Allow: That first factor of recognition is a game changer. However, if not followed by this second factor, that recognition may fade away in the clamor of associated sensations, memories, emotions, and thoughts. This factor is very difficult for most, especially those new to mindfulness or to anger management. Here we allow this experience, whatever it is, to be exactly as it is in this moment. We allow it to be. We accept the feeling, sensation, emotion, cognition, or situation. In 12-step recovery, there is a saying that "acceptance is the answer to all my problems today." In these programs, many people struggle with acceptance, feeling more attuned to the awareness of the first step and the action of the third step. You might feel that if you accept the anger or the associated sensations that it will run you over. That's the way it has been your whole life, or so it seems. The truth is that when surrounded by the other elements of RAIN, this becomes your opportunity to withstand the unpleasantness and then hold it in awareness until it changes. Addiction is a good example again. Many people use substances to either make a feeling go away or make it even more pronounced so that they can act out. Here is another option: Let the feeling come, recognize it is here, and allow it to remain in your conscious awareness. See if what you are working with, having been recognized, can now be allowed to be here, right now, as it is. Right now, it's like this.

Investigate: This third factor in the process is also critical. Perhaps if we stopped at simply allowing, the recognition would slip away still, and we would be vulnerable once again. We want to continue our process of mindfulness and dig a little deeper. By doing this we work on multiple levels. We deepen our concentration, which is a key to our mindfulness kit. We continue to lean in to our neocortex, the wise part of our mind, thus keeping it active and allowing us to see further into the truth of the impermanence of our current state of mind. We learn more about the sensation, emotion, cognition, or situation, and in learning more about it we become familiar in a way that will allow us to intervene even earlier the next time and with more equanimity. Instead of being swept away by the initial experience into a tidal wave of associated memories, thoughts, sensations, and beliefs, we utilize the grounding of *recognize* and *allow* to investigate more deeply the experience at hand. See if you can do that with the issue you are looking at right now. Having recognized it for what it is and allowed it to stay for a moment, investigate it with a spirit of curiosity. What is this?

Nurture: When this has all been done, you will have gone through a great deal. In some traditions of mindfulness, they speak of this being the work of a spiritual warrior. There is a reason for that. It takes a great deal of strength, courage, and energy just to decide to move into recognition. Anger and other strong emotions can be very compelling, and it seems easier to give in to the swarm of associated emotions, sensations, and cognitions. So, after a hard moment or hour or day of doing RAIN practice, we need to take care of ourselves. A large part of this process is the practice of self-compassion.

Compassion may seem like an overused word, but I have seen it underutilized when it comes to one's own self. Compassion is the acknowledgment of the suffering that we go through and then the application of whatever nurturing our mind, body, and spirit need. This can come through further direct mindfulness practices, especially practices like loving-kindness meditation, a practice in which we intentionally, in a focused manner, direct kind and loving thoughts toward ourselves. It can come through a physical act like exercise, a bath, relational mindfulness with a friend, or a yoga class. Sending ourselves compassion after doing this work stabilizes our nervous system and brings the recognition, the allowing, and the investigation to completion. We now have a visceral mindfulness experience that we may find more and more available over time and a more even keel to start with when the next strong emotion arises. See what nurturing you need after examining your current issue. How can you show yourself compassion at this moment? Below is an example scenario using the RAIN exercise.

Recognize

I am stewing over the fight I had last night on the phone with my friend.

Allow

I sat in meditation for five minutes and settled my breath and body just enough to be able to accept the feelings of hurt and the tension in my body.

Investigate

As I looked at my body tension, I saw that it was feeding my thoughts, and so I let go even further. I stopped rerunning the tape of the argument, and I had some insight into where I was at fault in the argument.

Nurture

I can let go of the argument and the feeling of it being so personal. I am going to do some writing to see how I can go back to my friend and apologize for my part in how it escalated, and then I will spend time with my dog.

Now try using the following space to track your own issue.

Recognize

_____

_____

_____

_____

Allow

_____

_____

_____

_____

Investigate

_____

_____

_____

_____

Nurture

_____

_____

_____

_____

You Are Not Your Anger

What is the purpose of RAIN practice and other mindfulness skills that deal directly with anger? They help you understand that your anger is a fleeting experience that you can choose to neutrally observe. It is not as daunting as it seems. Look back on your anger from 10 minutes ago. Where is it? How about 10 months ago? What were you angry about then? Ten years ago? Again, some of these angry feelings or ideas may persist, but upon further investigation, you can see how your feelings of anger as well as other strong feelings have arisen and then passed. Since we see that to be true, we can make that truth our friend and utilize it to make the choice of increasing our mindfulness. If we can recognize that our anger is a fleeting experience, then we can allow it in for its limited engagement, investigate it with openness and curiosity, and then nurture ourselves back to balance and some peace.

What is this skill of awareness doing for us? It is bringing us into the present moment. Anyone with familiarity with mental health treatment, positive psychology, mindfulness, or a wide variety of spiritual and religious traditions has been instructed to find a way to be in the moment. The value of the present moment sometimes eludes the beginning mindfulness practitioner. For ages, I may have found any way, shape, or form to help me escape the present moment. The truth, however, is that this moment is the only one in progress right now. The past has already passed, and the future is unknown and not here yet. Regret about the past and worry about the future take us out of our present-moment experience. They also can lead us into thoughts and feelings of anger. Traveling backward or forward in our minds takes us off point, out of mindfulness and awareness, and into the forest of what the Buddhists call "monkey mind," swinging from branch to branch of thought to thought to sensation to emotion and back to thought. In other words, past or future thinking can trigger us into anger and other strong emotions that are exacerbated by monkey mind. So, we want to attend to this present moment in order to stay in this present moment. What happens when we don't do this regularly?

LIVING IN THE PAST: OLD WOUNDS
AND PAST RESENTMENTS

When I was first introduced to 12-step recovery, I looked at the steps and saw that the fulcrum of the whole experience was the fourth step, making a "searching and fearless moral inventory." At the heart of this inventory was a list of resentments. In a sense, resentments are bouts of anger that are fostered and kept close until they morph into a permanent state of anger. Sometimes it can be burning nonstop; sometimes it is a low hum in the background of experience, coloring our current doings from a mostly unconscious place.

After a short time in Alcoholics Anonymous, I looked at the steps anew and noticed something. The 12 steps are essentially an anger management program. "Resentments are the number one offender," they say. That was a big wake-up call. Was it indeed true that management of my anger was going to be the key to all of my recovery, from addiction and otherwise? Today I am grateful that I met this type of recovery and mindfulness at the same time.

Buddha pointed out three poisons that affect human beings: greed, anger, and delusion. Anger lives in the middle of this dynamic as well as holding its own place, since when I don't get what I want I might get angry, when the thing I don't want doesn't go away I can become angry, and when my delusion proves a failure … you get the picture. So, this can be boiled down to "I want what I want," "I want to make what I don't want go away," and "I run around believing that if I can manage that particular binary, I will be happy."

So, what about these long-standing resentments? Some wounds are very deep and are the products of deep harm. Asking someone to just "let go" of those resentments cold turkey, without the right supports in place, can actually cause more harm. If you have resentments connected to old hurts that one would consider traumatic and are suffering symptoms of PTSD or other difficulties that arise from untreated emotional wounds, definitely seek professional help. This is not just my due diligence as a clinician covering my bases; this is my deeply felt professional advice based on personal and clinical experience.

That being said, now is a good time to begin initial work on long-standing resentments. Once these memories are at the level of conscious awareness, we can apply mindfulness to them just as we can to those difficulties that arise in the moment. I become aware of the resentment tied to the old hurt. I allow it to be as it is, as it has been, then I investigate it. I may find the threads that have tangled into a ball, and through revealing the elements of the resentment, I can heal the elements and the resentment as a whole. And I can take care of myself throughout this process and when I am finished with the work.

Here is a quick exercise you can do to start this process of letting go of resentments. Again, you don't have to go all the way to the deep end of the pool immediately in order to get this work done. Start with three to five resentments that are at the level you can handle at this moment. As you build resilience through this process, and as you develop your mindfulness skills, you will find yourself able to reprocess more and more of this material.

»»→ LETTING GO OF OLD WOUNDS AND PAST RESENTMENTS

This exercise uses the mindfulness skill of labeling to begin the process of letting go of the specific resentments we are holding. For this exercise, write down between three and five resentments that trigger your anger in the present moment. Next to the name of the person or institution, write down why the resentment is there.

RESENTMENT   REASON FOR RESENTMENT

_____   _____

_____   _____

_____   _____

_____   _____

_____   _____

_____   _____

   Now choose one of the resentments. Sit in a comfortable position, and bring that person or institution into your consciousness. Breathe as deeply as you can three times. Then give the person a general label, perhaps "resentment." Hold this word in your mind as their primary descriptor as you gently let the person go, as if they were a cloud passing in the sky. If the person refuses to move, as they might, gently try again. You might even put them in or on a physical cloud, label it "resentment," and then let it go. Check in with your body, and notice any differences in your physical sensations. See if there is any relief. If you have time and want to work with another resentment, feel free. As with any exercise like this, take care of yourself afterward in a way that feels healthy and adaptive.

ANGER AND FORGIVENESS

Embedded in the nature of anger and especially resentment is the dilemma of forgiveness. Many people struggle with forgiveness because they believe it is an event, a binary of "I forgive you" or "I don't forgive you." Many ancient and modern spiritual teachers, including mindfulness teachers, have touted the importance of forgiveness in the healing of anger, both long- and short-term.

Mindfulness helps us see forgiveness on a continuum, as a process rather than an event. Forgiveness can be something that we need to have for ourselves, for others, or for both. Often the cycle of anger involves our taking it out on others, resulting in anger at ourselves for doing that, followed by taking it out on others because of that pain followed by … again, you get the picture. Forgiveness can be applied at any point during this cycle. So, where you start is not important, whether it's self-forgiveness or forgiveness of the other. The important thing is that we develop the willingness to consider the possibility of forgiveness.

As with the previous exercise on letting go of resentments, we can start small. We don't have to forgive the worst of the worst in a knee-jerk and possibly superficial fashion to get the job done. We simply need to understand that even small thoughts and acts of forgiveness change the direction of our thoughts and intentions going forward. If I am able to forgive myself or another, I am now committed at least for the moment to think and act differently in relation to the pain. I can use all that I know about my own pain to perhaps understand the pain of the person who acted in a way that made me feel angry. And I can lean in to that same understanding of our common humanity to forgive myself for acting out in anger at others. It is human. I am in a process. And I can forgive myself as well as others, little by little, moment by moment. Over time, the forgiveness builds and can radiate outward toward other situations, other people, other aspects of myself.

SHAME

Besides the fear or aversion to forgiveness, another very powerful force that we need to contend with in our anger management work is shame. Think of shame as all that we believe as unforgiveable coagulated into a huge ball. We may even have a physical sensation of where that shame resides, triggered by a whole host of possible situations, people, or internal stress.

Although there exists what many spiritual and psychological teachers have called healthy shame, unhealthy shame can be the trigger for our anger. Shame can be thought of as the core set of lies and cognitive distortions built over time into concretized ideas about self as worthless, bad, not good enough, or any number of other negative beliefs. Shame is a dense and seemingly immovable version of distorted beliefs about self in the same way that resentment is a dense and seemingly immovable version of the anger response. Therefore, the journey of untangling shame through mindfulness and other practices will be for the long haul, and with our newfound mindfulness skills we can notice what the nature of our shame is, we can notice where it resides in our body and mind, and we can move forward with this process of anger management moment to moment while chipping away at the distortions of shame.

»»→ FORGIVENESS MEDITATION

The process of forgiveness can begin and be ushered along utilizing mind-fulness practice. The following short meditation can help you work on your forgiveness of self and others.

Sit in a comfortable position. Feel free to close your eyes, but also feel free to keep your eyes open if that feels more comfortable or grounding for you. If your eyes are open, have them half shut and downcast at a 45-degree angle, and just rest your gaze on the spot in front of you. Take three deep breaths, as deep as you are able. Notice the sensations of your body against surfaces, your back against the chair, feet on the floor, any other points of contact. Let yourself notice any of those points that feel grounded. If you don't feel grounded, notice that with as little judgment as possible.

Now bring to mind the person you wish to forgive. Notice any changes in your body sensations as you do so. When you are ready, in your mind silently say to this person, "I forgive you for your unskillful actions that I felt to be harmful. I realize your pain is like mine. I forgive you." Take a couple of breaths, noticing any changes in your body. Repeat the phrase as many times as you need. Feel free to keep this meditation short, five minutes or less, until you feel ready to go longer. To adjust this meditation toward self, do the same setup, but change the phrase to "I forgive myself for my unskill-ful thoughts and actions that have caused myself and others suffering. I realize my pain and anger is a human response. I forgive myself."

Being Here Now

Let's go back to this idea of being in the present moment. Why does staying in the present moment help heal and manage anger? The greatest stressors we have available are in fact lurking in the past and looming in the future. If we are able to place ourselves in the present moment experience, then we have to deal only with the situations, sensations, people, and internal emotional and cognitive experiences of this very moment. As soon as we start stacking blocks of the past on top of the present moment and worriedly constructing new structures of the future that we cannot predict anyway, we are making the present moment that much more complicated. Sometimes we can get to the point where we literally eradicate our awareness of the present moment experience.

Focusing on the past and/or future makes us vulnerable to a whole host of anger triggers that we can find in our regrets from the past and our anxiety about the future. Focusing on the present moment helps us keep our task at hand limited to the moment's activities. It can also help us to keep our cognitive abilities online so that they may provide a counterpoint to the fight or flight response or any negative spin that comes up in the moment. *Be here now* is not just some hippie speak from a long-gone era. *Be here now* becomes the central organizing principle of mindful anger management.

PRESENT MOMENT EXPERIENCE

I feel fortunate to have done Zen meditation training for so long. There is an incredibly strong encouragement to get out of the discursive thoughts of the mind and to drop into the present moment experience in the body. Zen monks and nuns call it *training* for a reason. It is a retraining of the brain. It is a workout that changes the focus of our energy and the use of our energy. Just noticing the workings of the breath and body is a simple and effective way to come into the present moment, to allow the past and future to fall away. This is not to say that our memories are not useful for learning and for internal resourcing and resilience, or that we should forsake planning forever and just march along from moment to moment. It is to say that our default can change from being in the past and future monkey mind to being in the present moment experience, and then we can go to past and future from that more skillful place.

The implications for anger management are immense. In this moment, I can maintain awareness of my emotional states, including anger, and I can stay with them from moment to moment and watch them change, transform, and fall away. Over time, it becomes a very peaceful preemptive strike on our anger response.

The next exercise offers a short meditation that can help you access the present moment; you can do it any time you feel yourself drifting out of the moment and into anger.

⟫⟫→ BEING IN THE PRESENT MOMENT MEDITATION

This exercise is a meditation where you may write down your experience of the present moment using the five senses. Try it now.

What does this book feel like in your hand?

_____

_____

What is the sensation of the pages on your fingertips?

_____

_____

How are you sitting?

_____

_____

Notice the sensation of your breath. Is the air cold or warm as it enters your nostrils?

_____

_____

What colors do you see?

_____

_____

Are there any sounds in the room?

_____

_____

It may not seem like much, but this kind of awareness practice is actually training your mind and body to be more centered. The idea is that with practice, you become aware of anger and less and less fused with it over time, and your ability to let it go will grow.

⏩➤ TRIGGERING EVENTS MONITOR

Below is a chart for you to mark any triggering events and track how you're feeling and what you're thinking during the events. We will repeat this exercise throughout the book as a way to build awareness of your anger, your reactions, your responses and to track your progress.

DATE/TIME	TRIGGER	TRIGGER INTENSITY: 0–10	THOUGHTS	ACTIONS	BODY SENSATIONS

Final Thoughts

In this chapter, we learned that we are not our anger. Once we have that initial understanding we can step back and work with our anger. By applying mindfulness, we recognize anger when it arises, we allow it to be what it is, and we look deeply into its nature and find ourselves less likely to act on it. Then we can nurture ourselves, rewarding ourselves for being in this process and setting the stage for more resilience, more insight, and more skills to work with our anger rather than being worked over by it.

CHAPTER 4

Healing the Angry Body

A mindfulness teacher told me over and over again that mindfulness practice is not a practice of the mind—it is a practice of the body. Becoming aware of how anger feels in the body is where we will find our answers and our alternative strategies. It may seem counterintuitive to discuss body before mind, but when it comes to anger, it is really beneficial to tap into the body. We can actually bring awareness away from the mind, where we tend to be comfortably fixed, cycling through our angry thoughts, mindlessly getting caught in them.

The practice of bringing attention elsewhere in the body can help break that anger cycle and offer powerful healing. Oftentimes when we're in anger, we are quite outside the body. We are ruminating or growing agitated. An important step in overcoming anger is to connect with the physical sensations of the emotions so that we can have greater control of them, become aware of when anger is coming on, and avoid acting on it.

Bringing Mindful Awareness to the Body

Many of my psychotherapy clients who identify anger management as one of their issues will either report difficulty with knowing what they are feeling in the body or demonstrate behaviors that are in place to desensitize the body in some way. Stress placed on the body has now been implicated in everything from having a difficult day to developing cancer and other chronic or fatal diagnoses. The stress response in the body and the anger response for the most part are one and the same on a biological level. Stress and anger can manifest in body-related distress such as chronic pain or ulcers, or we might self-medicate them away with drugs and alcohol or addictive behaviors.

A great deal of what is taught in mindfulness practice and in anger management in general seems counterintuitive. As a suffering person, it would make sense that one would want to escape from the awareness of pain and difficulty in order to ease the suffering. However, that turns out to be a short-term strategy with long-term consequences if used over and over again. Buddha made it very clear through his long career of teaching that to address our pain, we need to lean into it and become familiar with it. We need to bring awareness to this experience of being human. Mindfulness teachers over the millennia have offered a number of ways to bring attention to the body and through that attention bring awareness, and through that awareness bring new perspectives, intentions, and actions. Here is a quick exercise utilizing the breath as the anchor to start our journey of healing the angry body.

⫸➤ PRACTICE: QUICK BREATH AWARENESS

This exercise is designed to help you notice the basic mechanics of your breath. The breath represents our best tracker of the moment and a bridge to awareness of the body. Before we can become aware of what's going on inside, let's first become aware of our breath. As discussed in the previous chapter, getting into the moment is a key to managing our anger. We can go to our breath at any time to check in and see how we are doing and how our body is responding to current conditions. Awareness of the breath will also allow us some agency in working with our body actively to relieve stress and anger.

No need to get into a comfortable position here or light a candle. This is something you can do anywhere, anytime. Find a spot just outside your nostrils or just inside your nostrils. If you are stuffed up, try this with your mouth instead. Focus keenly on that spot. Take in a breath and notice its quality. Let the breath out, doing the same. As you continue breathing, notice several qualities. Is my breath short or long? Deep or shallow? Does the air feel cool or warm? Is it pleasant, unpleasant, or neutral? Does it feel like it is going into my chest or further down into my belly? Check on all of these aspects of the breath, and if you feel like you can slow down your breathing or deepen it, go ahead and do that for yourself.

YOUR BODY AND BRAIN ON ANGER

Anger is a biological response. Fight or flight is a dance between two parts of our brain dedicated to maintaining safety and survival. The most reactive and primitive part of the brain we share with the reptiles, and it is highly reactive to stimulation. There is a stimulus activating fight or flight, and we react.

The paleomammalian brain is more sophisticated and brings emotion into the picture as a more developed response system. These systems are designed to release cortisol, adrenaline, and other hormones to engage in battle. When activated to a high degree, the third part of our brain, where the cognitive abilities unique to humans are located, literally shuts down. Blood flow can stop in some areas. That is why so many people will say they do not remember what happened when they were angry or they don't know why they acted the way they did. There is biological truth to that in many cases. That's why this work is so critical.

⇒⇒→ PRACTICE: BODY SCAN

In the previous exercise we investigated the breath. Another option is to bring that sense of awareness to the rest of the body. This exercise is a classic from many traditions ancient and modern, where we touch on what is happening throughout our body in order to bring the whole body into awareness.

You can do this exercise in any posture, whether standing, seated, or lying down. We are going to scan our body and identify sensations from the top of our head to the bottoms of our feet. First settle into the chosen posture. Take a few breaths, with a general awareness of your body, letting the breaths come as deeply as you are able in this moment. Now go ahead and focus your attention on your scalp. See if you can truly zero in on this part of your body. If this feels difficult, remember this is a process, and see if you can notice your difficulty with the exercise with as little judgment as possible in this moment. See what is present in the scalp. Hold this attention for a few seconds, and then shift downward to the temples. Remember to bring the focus in as keenly as you can. Then we will work our way down. As we go to the cheeks, the eyes, the nose, the mouth, and the chin one by one, what are we noticing? Is there any pain? Any clenching? Or are we already relaxed? Is there tingling? Are the sensations that we notice pleasant, unpleasant, or neutral?

We continue down the rest of the body, both noticing and inquiring into each part of our body. The neck and throat ... the shoulders ... the arms and hands ... the chest and upper back ... the stomach and lower back ... the pelvis and the seat ... the legs ... all the way down to the feet. When you are done, check in with your breath and see if its quality has changed. If you find yourself more relaxed than when you began, you can scan in a general way for any residual discomfort or stress and bring that more relaxed energy toward the stressed part. This gives you the opportunity to not only increase your awareness through the body scan but to use its benefits immediately to bring a greater involvement in your own care of your anger and stress.

Common Physiological Signs of Anger

Acute stress, anger, and anger-triggering events are among the body's top stressors, and when they occur the body's sympathetic nervous system is activated due to the release of hormones. The sympathetic nervous system stimulates the adrenal glands and triggers the release of adrenaline and noradrenaline. This results in an increase in heart rate, blood pressure, and breathing rate. After the threat is gone, it will take between 20 and 60 minutes for the body to return to its pre-arousal levels. As a result of this hormonal change, you will often notice:

- Your heart rate will increase.

- Your vision may narrow.

- Your muscles may become tense.

- You may begin to sweat.

- Your hearing may become more sensitive.

This is all due to physiological changes designed to aid in fight or flight:

- **Heightened sensitivity:** Blood flow to the surface of the body is reduced so that the blood flow to the arms, legs, shoulders, brain, eyes, ears, and nose can be increased. Besides getting ready to run and fight, the body is preparing to think quickly and be aware of threats by hearing, seeing, and smelling things better.

- **Sweating:** Highly charged activity will cause an increase in body heat. To prepare for that, the body starts to sweat as soon as it feels stressed in order to cool off our system.

- **Dilated pupils:** To let more light in and improve sight, the pupils dilate.

- **Dry mouth:** Gastric juices and saliva production decrease because blood flow to the digestive system is decreased. This is about priorities in the moment. It's more important to survive in this moment than to digest our food. This same reaction also can cause an upset stomach in the moment, and, when triggered, often brings chronic stomach distress.

All of these sympathetic nervous system responses may bring other identifiable changes in posture or movement, including accelerated breathing, balled fists, flaring nostrils, pacing, or increased decibel levels while speaking.

When you're angry, your body is literally preparing to do whatever it takes to help you survive a threat. As if you were in the wild, running from a bear, your body does these things to help you. But because you no longer live in the wild, it's within your power to manage these evolved reactions, to take back some control and determine what is an actual bear and what is non-life-threatening anger or frustration.

EXPRESSING ANGER

If we were to boil down the issue of anger management to its essence, it would be this: How do we express our anger in a healthy way? Anger manifests in the body through fight or flight and the related responses that it expresses in our psyche with thoughts and emotional content. Anger is energy filled with action potential. It is completely natural for it to come about. It cannot just disappear as much as we would like it to—it needs to be expressed.

When the fight or flight system kicks in, the body will do what fight or flight tells it to do regardless of what rational thought has to say. That is why our mindfulness journey is so crucial. Mindfulness is our ongoing and proactive decision to try to stay one step ahead of our anger expression so that we might be able to have a say in the expression. One reason we do this is so that we can honor the normalcy of the emotion, staying aware of its functionality. It is providing us with boundary setting and safety; it is energy that advocates for us and others.

When we are angry, there is a highly functional component. When, then, does it become dysfunctional? We can chalk it up to an ongoing lack of mindfulness, whereby the anger response in our body is allowed to run wild. What happens for many of us is that the angry body gets triggered and retriggered, and the memory information from the event is not stored in the long-term memory where it can be accessed, made sense of, and recognized as something that happened in the past. It can get stuck in the anger-centered parts of the brain and body, so when new situations come up that are similar either externally or internally, the person will respond similarly. This builds up a network of anger-laden reactions that continually reinforce each other. The discomfort of this leads to a need to either discharge the energy through action or engage in behaviors or thought processes designed to numb the system. This is where the expression of anger turns dysfunctional. Again, it is not the anger that is the problem. It is our opinion about the anger combined with our expression of it that goes above and beyond our actual needs, avoids the feelings through some kind of substance or behavior, and/or does harm of some kind to ourselves or others.

⟫⟫→ DYSFUNCTIONAL EXPRESSIONS OF ANGER

Here is a checklist of some examples of possible dysfunctional expressions of anger. This list is not all-inclusive, and the issue is not cookie-cutter. There are some blank lines included for you to add any that you do not see on the list but feel that you engage in. Some of the items on the list are general examples; some items are more specific. Some items are obvious dysfunctional acting-out examples; others are the outward manifestations of anger that is being repressed. Feel free to check any that are part of your own experience and write in some of your own if you don't see them on this list.

ACTING OUT

❏ **Aggression**

❏ **Yelling**

❏ **Punching a wall**

❏ **Cutting someone off in traffic**

❏ **Pursuing someone who cut you off in traffic**

❏ **Mocking**

❏ **Bullying**

❏ **Breaking dishes**

❏ **Threatening body language**

❏ **Sarcasm**

❏ **Frequent sighing**

❏ **Overcontrolled tone of voice**

❏ **Sleep problems—too much or too little**

❏ **Irritability**

❏ **Ongoing clenched jaw or teeth grinding**

❏ _____

❏ _____

❏ _____

❏ _____

❏ _____

OUTWARD MANIFESTATIONS OF REPRESSED ANGER

❏ Lethargy

❏ Chronic depression

❏ Substance abuse

❏ Addictive behaviors

❏ Procrastination

❏ Habitual lateness

❏ Self-harm

❏ _____

❏ _____

❏ _____

❏ _____

❏ _____

Reacting Mindfully

Mindfulness teachers and psychologists are in agreement that there is a difference between reacting and responding. Reacting can be thought of as responding from the parts of the brain we share with the animal kingdom, the highly reactive reptilian brain and the more developed limbic brain containing our emotions, attachment behaviors, and a more advanced fight or flight response system. Responding comes from an interplay between our human cognitive abilities and our emotional and reactive systems. Mindfulness can be our guide in both instances. As an intervention it can be there in the short term to help keep our reactions as harmless as possible. Mindfulness does not have to wait for chaos to set in to then try to do damage control. Developing this skill allows us to intervene earlier and earlier in the anger cycle as it progresses from body responses to thought processes to acting out or acting in.

What does it look like to react mindfully and to intervene earlier in the anger cycle? You can use your ongoing Anger Check-in Scale as a guidepost. At what number did you feel out of control when you first started doing the exercise? Now consider your resting anger rate. This is the baseline anger that you start your day with and that follows you throughout your day. On a scale of 0 to 10, what was your resting anger rate today? Were you waking up at a high level of anger without even getting out of bed? When we are practicing mindfulness and are able to get the general level of anger down, we are providing a cushion for those instances when our anger is triggered so that it will take less energy to bring mindfulness into our reaction. And when we are able to become more distress tolerant and stay more mindful even at the higher numbers of our anger scale, we are able to keep our cognitive abilities online sufficiently to interact with our body-driven anger reactions.

Again, mindfulness is an act of bringing awareness to your present moment experience. This awareness is achieved by being fully in the present, but that is achieved by being able to detach healthily from the emotions that are present. This is not about surgery but rather taking just a small step back, enough so you might be able to tune in to the fact that you are in strong emotions in the moment when you are in anger. When you can do this, you are able to have some agency over your reactions.

At the same time, you can become aware of the fact that you are not a one-trick pony, even when you are angry. We can tune in to parts of our experience outside the immediate anger reactions. When I am working with people on their anxiety, often I will instruct them to find a part of their body that is not anxious at the moment, perhaps the elbow. This might apply to anger as well.

Another set of ancient exercises to help us tune in to different internal experiences are the heart practices of loving-kindness, compassion, appreciative joy, and equanimity. Buddha taught that these qualities would be the end result of practice, but he also suggested they could be cultivated actively with effort. Loving-kindness is the qualities of goodwill and interconnectedness that we can summon up and radiate out to others. Compassion is that feeling of deep concern regarding the suffering of others and can include action toward the ending of their suffering. Appreciative joy occurs when you see others happy and successful but do not feel envious; rather, you feel joy because of their joy. Equanimity is when you are able to maintain qualities of calm and balance even in the face of difficult situations.

There are many ways to look into your heart to find sensations and feelings there that are different from anger reactions and can provide healing in the moment and over the long term. What follows is a short-form version of the four major heart practices combined– loving-kindness, compassion, appreciative joy, and equanimity.

⟫⟩→ MEDITATION: BRINGING AWARENESS TO YOUR HEART

This meditation brings your awareness to the heart instead of the mind or other stimulated parts of the body—a quick, calming practice.

If it helps you, you can place your hand or both hands over your heart for this exercise, bringing deeper connection and physical warmth to this part of your body. Find a comfortable position that you feel is sustainable, or if you are doing this on the fly—for instance, in the middle of a crowded room—lean your weight into your feet so you feel more firmly grounded, to give you a starting point for your heart practice.

Bring your attention to your heart area, and send loving-kindness to yourself by saying this phrase silently in your mind: "May I be free from fear." (The heart practices described by Buddhist teachers often involve repeating phrases silently.) Then bring someone to mind you feel compassion toward—you feel for their pain. Send compassion to them with this silent phrase: "May you be free from fear." Bring up someone you know is doing well, and your heart is made glad by their good fortune. Send them appreciative joy with this phrase, said silently: "I am so glad you are free from fear." Now bring equanimity to your experience by silently saying, "May I be at ease."

You can do this meditation for five minutes or make it shorter or longer as needed. You can focus on scrolling through all four heart practices, or you can pick one or two to focus on in any given practice session. As you say the phrases, keep your attention on the heart area, and check back into that area after each phrase. What you are doing in this practice is bringing the attention to these possible aspects of your experience that are different from the parts of your body that are activated by the anger. This mindful attention to the whole of your experience, including the angry body states and the healing heart states, allows you to engage in more choice in your reaction to whatever situation is triggering you in the moment.

THE CHOICE POINT

Viktor Frankl, the great 20th-century psychiatrist, spoke of the moment between thought and action as the key to all mindful response. The pause that comes before action can make the difference between acting out and responding mindfully. This is perhaps the most important skill that we will develop: finding the pause and acting on it. The pause is where we can acknowledge our body sensations and emotional energy related to our anger and see them for what they are—natural reactions awaiting our response. This is where we get to choose between functional and dysfunctional responses.

⋙⟶ Emergency Tip

When you notice one of your triggers coming up or one of your typical body responses to anger, take immediate action to find the pause. Finding the pause is not finding the next intervention. It is the precursor to whatever response you are going to have. So, if walking away is not an option, then you need to find your best method for providing with your heart and mind similar results to those you get from walking away. Sense your feet on the ground. Choose a breath-tracking point at the nostrils or the belly. Notice any thoughts going through your mind and label them as thoughts. And then sense where the anger is in your body. Label it appropriately as hot or cold, dense or shallow, long or short. Then come back to your heart or where you find ground. You have now paused long enough to begin to assess the next response.

RESPONDING MINDFULLY

Reacting comes straight from the body processes and into action. Responding is what can come after the pause. Our mindfulness is something we develop so that we might get out ahead of our immediate reactions. That same quality can be applied to our responses after the pause. All of our higher-level human abilities can come into play here—our abilities to assess, utilize life lessons from the past, make meaning, use good judgment regarding outcomes, and make skillful decisions that will be harmless or reduce harm.

One way to cultivate the ability to respond mindfully is to come up with some simple ways to calm yourself down. I once had a guide in my life whose answer to all the problems I brought to him started with "the first thing you need to do is calm down." Everyone has a different idea of what is calming to the central nervous system. Finding your own calming activities is key. A friend told me that anything at all, large or small, that is healthy or adaptive can go on the list. He asked me if I liked the minty fresh taste in my mouth after brushing my teeth. I said yes. He said, "Put it on the list." Here are a few examples and some space for you to add your own.

Calming Activities:

- Brush my teeth
- Clean a small section of the house
- Rub my eyes
- Take a shower or bath
- Pet an animal
- Read a book for pleasure
- _____
- _____
- _____
- _____
- _____

➤➤→ TRIGGERING EVENTS MONITOR

It's time to consider recent triggering events and track how you were feeling and what you were thinking during the events. Again, this is a way to build awareness of your anger, your reactions, and your responses and to track your progress.

DATE/TIME	TRIGGER	TRIGGER INTENSITY: 0–10	THOUGHTS	ACTIONS	BODY SENSATIONS

⇒⇒→ ANGER CHECK-IN

You've made it through another chapter, so let's do a spot check on your current anger. See where your anger is right now, in this moment, on a scale of 0 to 10. Notice why you think you are at your current number. Notice if you have found yourself changing since beginning the book, and consider whether you have a clearer picture of what your number is on a regular basis. Notice if your resting anger rate is lowering. Mark your number on the scale below and use the lines below it to write a few thoughts as to why you are at that number.

0   1   2   3   4   5   6   7   8   9   10

Final Thoughts

In this chapter, we looked at how anger affects the body and how the body drives the anger response. In order to get this anger management job done, we need to bring awareness to the body so that we might get ahead of the body's automatic and natural tendency to do what it needs to do to survive. Once we have this greater awareness of our body processes, we have increased agency over them and the ability to harness our power of reason to work on the anger in the mind.

CHAPTER 5

Healing the Angry Mind

In this chapter we will begin to understand the cognitive and mental cycles of anger by investigating how our thoughts feed anger. We will explore ways to develop a healthier communication with self and others as well as how to respond to triggers more skillfully.

Bringing Mindful Awareness to Thoughts

Whether we are talking about anger or some other aspect of life, our goal of bringing awareness to our experience starts with the body and then moves on to this problem of the mind. In a core teaching of mindfulness, the historical Buddha spoke of starting with the foundation of mindfulness of body states. That is why we addressed the body first in this book. The mind is too complex a web of thoughts and feelings for many people to be able to start there and just go ahead and change their mind states. It is why body-based psychotherapies are becoming more popular, as we realize that until and unless we come to an understanding and an awareness of our biological systems, we may not be able to settle our minds.

You don't have to become a meditation master living at a monastery on top of a mountain to qualify to move on to this chapter. If you have started your practice of the exercises in this book or have simply been reading and absorbing, you probably have sufficient mindfulness of your body to begin to reorganize your mind.

Similar to our work with the body, we need to become aware of some of the common signs and symptoms of anger at work in the mind. We also need to come up with mindfulness strategies that are particular to dealing with the complicated nature of our thought processes. Our goal in this work will be to acknowledge that thought precedes action, and so this is our next potential area of intervention. Awareness of the body helps us intervene in and dial down our biological anger responses. Awareness of our thinking helps us not exacerbate those biological responses with thoughts that only grow the anger.

Common Cognitive Signs of Anger

- "Seeing red"
- Rumination
- Racing thoughts
- Panic
- Thoughts of hurting someone
- Wanting to teach someone a lesson
- Believing someone is rude on purpose
- Thinking about seeking revenge
- Believing something bad is happening
- Mind going blank

WISE MIND

Wise mind describes the mind state we are working toward in our mindfulness-based anger management work. Wise mind in fact honors the emotionally driven mind, that part of us that is designed to protect and intuitively guide us and includes anger as part of its integral makeup. In order for this mind to be wise, however, it needs to link up to the rational mind. When our instincts for survival are able to guide and be guided by our human rationality, that is when we are able to have agency over our thoughts and actions.

The teachings of Buddha included a teaching known as *not-self*, which can be translated here as *wise mind*, or not taking things so personally. We are able to step just a little bit apart from our ego, which takes us out of the potential for anger, since anger requires us to be focused on our self and our needs and our wants. In wise mind, we are using mindfulness to bring awareness to the neutral nature of body and mind so that we can develop the habit of soothing our nervous system, which allows our rational mind to participate in an ongoing relationship with our anger.

)))⟶ Emergency Tip

We are in a steady stream of self and other analysis at all times. It is a natural function of life. We are seeing ourselves in the world, and we are analyzing or judging all that we see. If you find yourself in rumination, step away from your mind by engaging in a body activity or a creative activity. Exercise, dance, run, do walking meditation. Anything that takes you into the body may distract you from the mind. You can also grab art materials or a journal. Here it may change from internal verbal venting to action on your own behalf, which changes the direction of your mind.

DEFUSING THOUGHTS

One of the greatest myths about mindfulness practice is that it is designed to completely clear your mind, and if you have not done so within your first five minutes of meditation you have failed. There are stories of spiritual masters with minds that are like a cloudless sky, still and peaceful to the point of bliss and tranquility. This is not required for you to get relief and transform your anger. Even the spiritual masters tell stories of achieving these blissful states and then getting angry when those states inevitably pass. And then they practice some more on that anger and come to their next conclusions.

Rather than clearing the mind until it's completely empty, we will be working on developing a new relationship to our thoughts that is more objective. The way people get to that calm place is not by zapping their thought processes into submission but rather through observing them. We can step back and watch the thoughts like a movie, rather than being the star of the movie. Just that act starts defusing the power of the thoughts. Then, if we are able to maintain this type of objective attention for a more sustained period, the effects continue to build. We don't end up in a dial-tone state but rather are more aware, focused, and able to address strong emotions like our anger.

➤➤➤ MEDITATION: WATCHING THOUGHTS GO BY

In this exercise you will bring up an anger-inducing situation in your mind's eye and then internally de-escalate it by utilizing mindfulness skills.

First find a comfortable position and choose whether you would like your eyes open or gently closed. Check in with your body and notice the points of contact with your chair or cushion. If you like, take three deep breaths, and then return to your normal breathing pattern.

Think back to a time when you experienced anger, something that happened relatively recently. You don't need to choose your worst episode. It may work better, in fact, to choose something that is charged but not overwhelming. Bring up the event and allow yourself to feel the anger again right now. Allow the feeling to get as strong as possible without becoming overwhelmed.

Other emotions, such as sadness or fear, may arise as you remember the episode. See if you can note them, maybe label them, and return to feeling the anger.

Start to notice thoughts that come up in relation to the anger. As you notice a thought arise, place the label of "thought" upon it and see if you can watch it go by like a cloud in the sky. Go ahead and continue to do this with thoughts as they arise. Every minute or so, check in with your body and mind to see if there has been any shift in the anger. If angry thoughts continue, use the labels and the clouds to have them drift by.

You might try bringing a sense of kindness and compassion to your anger. The feeling of anger is normal, part of being human. We all experience it at times. Thich Nhat Hanh suggested we might see if we can cradle our own anger like a mother cradling a newborn. What happens if you hold it in this way, with tenderness and care?

To complete this meditation, say good-bye to the event, the thoughts, and the feelings. Gently bring your attention back to the breath and stay with it for a while, letting your emotions settle into the spaciousness of your breath and awareness.

You can do this exercise to detach from angry thoughts when they arise or as a regular mindfulness practice.

Cognitive Distortions That Can Lead to or Escalate Anger

Cognitive distortions are a clinical way of describing the dysfunctional thought process of thinking and believing things that are not true. While mindfulness can help us detach from unhelpful thoughts, looking at our thoughts for what they are can also be helpful. There are several types of cognitive distortions, and you may identify with some of these ways of thinking:

Filtering: The negative details of a situation or a person are the only thing noticed and are ruminated upon.

Polarized Thinking (or "Black and White" Thinking): This or that, yes or no, my way or the highway.

Personalization: Everything you do or say is a very personal reaction to me.

Blaming: Other people and situations are responsible for my difficulties.

Shoulds: I myself, and all you others, should behave in a way that I believe to be the correct way.

Always Being Right: I must continually make sure to spend sufficient time convincing you that I am right.

Heaven's Reward Fallacy: We expect our sacrifice and self-denial to pay off, as if someone is keeping score. We feel bitter when the reward doesn't come.

When you read these types of thinking patterns or cognitive distortions, it's probably easy to see, when you're not in the heat of the moment, how they are unbalanced and, well... distorted. It's easy to see how they might lead to more anger and add more fuel to the fire.

You can actually combat these kinds of thinking patterns simply by reframing the distorted thoughts. With practice, just as you did with labeling thoughts in the earlier exercise, you can learn to take a step back, recognize that a cognition or thought was a distorted one, and then go ahead and edit that thought in a much more balanced and fair way that should help de-escalate the situation or negative thought spiral you find yourself in.

Reframing Hot Thoughts

Reframing is about looking at thoughts, actions, situations, and problems through a new prism, generating a new perspective. As we now well know, mindfulness itself is a millennia-old reframing device. By concentrating on the present moment and staying out of the past and future, we take the energy out of cognitive distortions, which need past and future tripping the way we need air and water. We utilize mindfulness to point us toward the present and pull us out of past and future analysis, and we are gifted with the peace of mind to be able to reframe. Here are short descriptions of what the mindful reframing of our original list of cognitive distortions would look like.

Filtering: We can see that not everything is negative, that there is pleasant and unpleasant and we can sit with both.

Polarized Thinking (or "Black and White" Thinking): We can get out of the binary and into the wider vista.

Personalization: It's not personal when you cut me off in traffic.

Blaming: I need to take a look at all situations and assess where I have a part. I don't deny the part of others, but I don't place all the blame on them.

Shoulds: I am not the arbiter of what people should and shouldn't do. I can control only my own thoughts and actions.

Always Being Right: Would I rather be right or be happy? I choose happy.

Heaven's Reward Fallacy: I can take all my actions and let go of the results. I can do all I do in the spirit of service, giving without expectation to receive.

⫸⟶ DOWNWARD ARROW TECHNIQUE

The downward arrow technique comes from cognitive behavioral therapy but has much in common with the investigatory aspect of mindfulness. The third foundation of mindfulness described by Buddha was mindfulness of mind. In insight meditation, one is encouraged to investigate thought processes to get to the root. In the downward arrow technique, we are encouraged to take a difficult situation, in this case perhaps something that makes us angry, and continue to ask "why" and "what" questions until we get to a core belief. This is an exercise to gain insight into the thinking process and see that many of our thoughts and beliefs aren't based in reality but instead fueled by cognitive distortions, and it's not until we investigate every layer of this thinking process that we finally are able to reveal the one truth beneath all the distortions. Even if it's a painful truth, it's worth discovering because only then can we come to a conclusion as to what would be a better action to take than acting out our anger. Here is an example:

This food I made for my family is terrible.

If that were true, what would it mean?

I am a terrible cook.

If that were true, what would it mean?

I am a bad parent and spouse.

If that were true, what would it mean?

My spouse will leave me.

If that were true, what would it mean?

I will be alone.

If that were true, what would it mean?

I am a failure.

The last statement is the core belief. If we are able to get at the core beliefs through this mindful investigation, we can start to heal them and have a better chance of developing more mindful responses to anger. We can address these core beliefs directly. In the space below, take a current or recent anger scenario and run it through the downward arrow.

_____

_____

_____

_____

If that were true, what would it mean?

_____

_____

_____

If that were true, what would it mean?

_____

_____

⬇

If that were true, what would it mean?

_____

_____

_____

_____

⬇

If that were true, what would it mean?

_____

_____

_____

_____

⬇

If that were true, what would it mean?

_____

_____

_____

_____

When you have found the core belief associated with your investigation, see if you can find a more reasonable expectation or belief that you can counter it with and write it here:

_____

_____

_____

_____

Communicating Mindfully

Mindfulness is not all about what is going on inside us. It includes our relationships and communication. Many see mindfulness as a way of life that includes our speech, our actions, and our livelihood. Speech does include internal speech. Many of us find ourselves talking to ourselves about ourselves in a manner that we would never allow anyone else to do. We also fall prey to the internal monologue's negative skew and end up on a monkey mind journey to cognitive distortions and worse. These distortions hook in to body sensations related to anger and body and mind material from previous unprocessed memories to create a possible wave of anger. So our internal speech needs to be addressed through our investigation steeped in an attitude of kindness toward ourselves.

When it comes to communicating with others, we can apply the same principle of leading with a kind attitude that also includes curiosity, open-ness, and assuming a reasonable amount of goodwill. Communication that involves anger issues is often a matter of conflict resolution. Much like anger, conflict gets a bad rap due to how destructive it can seem. The truth is that conflict is even more natural and abundant than anger itself. Conflict is a part of our moment-to-moment experience. We are constantly in a state of conflict that needs resolution. So coming to com-munication with others in the spirit of mindfulness, kindness, and conflict resolution can go a long way in not only de-escalating anger but even in stopping the anger response from arising in the first place.

Some basic communication skills to abide by when working through our anger management program are:

- Really listen.
- Don't interrupt.
- Assume goodwill.
- Don't yell, scream, or name call.
- Use a calm or neutral tone of voice.
- Refrain from putting others down.

- Don't try to mind read or assume you know what others think.
- Watch your negative body language, like rolling your eyes or focusing on other things.
- Don't blame others.
- Use "I" statements.

  Some basic conflict resolution skills to abide by are:
- Address problems quickly before they become a crisis.
- Assert feelings without blaming.
- Brainstorm solutions that accommodate both parties.
- Compromise to accommodate others.
- Commit to resolving problems.
- Be creative in problem-solving.

LISTENING

Listening is a key component of communication, and listening mindfully is an effective tool for better communication. Mindfulness has been defined by Jon Kabat-Zinn and other teachers as nonjudgmental present-moment awareness. This has extensive applications in the realm of listening.

Listening without judgment or expectation is an art and a skill that can be learned. In a variety of training sessions that I have done, we've used an activity where we have participants form concentric circles, one within the other, with each person facing another in the opposite circle. We then ask them questions to answer one at a time. The instruction we give to the listeners is to not give any feedback, verbal or nonverbal. Don't nod your head in agreement or say "I know what you mean"; try not to give away too much or any of your reaction to what the person is saying. This is not a natural way that we tend to communicate, but it can have great results as an exercise. It allows us to see that sometimes when we insert ourselves with a statement of our own, we have misunderstood the person because they had in fact only arrived at a comma that we thought was the period at the end of the sentence.

This shows us that our listening has to be more about, well, listening. How often, when someone is talking, are we busy formulating our opinion and response to what the other person is saying? When we are in this mode, we are certainly not in the moment. At the very least we are in the future, as we plan our future words of wisdom in response. Wise listening is listening deeply to the person before us and giving them the time and the space to explain themselves. This is all critical in anger management. A huge aspect of anger and conflict is misunderstanding. When we don't listen deeply, there is a greater chance of misunderstanding.

ASSERTIVENESS

Another key component of communication is our ability to be assertive. When you are assertive, you behave confidently and say what you want or believe in a direct way. How can we be assertive without being aggressive?

Skillful mindfulness can help you become assertive rather than aggressive. *Aggressiveness* describes a majority of the states of mind and action that one would define as anger. People get aggressive when there seems to be no other way to solve a problem or set a boundary. One of the major reasons that people become aggressive is they do not have the assertiveness skills to help them get their needs met. So assertiveness is the antidote to aggression. Many people have a hard time noting the difference.

Assertiveness is the act of wise mind. The rational mind and the emotional mind work together to determine reasonable needs and then make statements and take actions to get the needs met. Aggression is made up solely from the emotional mind and body states. Aggression cannot hear the voice of reason because it is being drowned out by the fight or flight response. Once we develop assertiveness, aggression becomes unnecessary. Assertiveness works with our attitudes of kindness, curiosity, and openness to help us get our needs met without any aggression entering the picture. And as a result, we get our needs met rather than suffer the consequences of aggression.

➤➤➤ TRIGGERING EVENTS MONITOR

Take a moment to consider the past week and mark any triggering events on the chart below. We will continue this exercise throughout the book to build awareness of your anger, your reactions, and your responses and to track your progress.

DATE/TIME	TRIGGER	TRIGGER INTENSITY: 0–10	THOUGHTS	ACTIONS	BODY SENSATIONS

Final Thoughts

In this chapter, we investigated the nature of our thoughts, particularly those that lead to anger and come from anger. Bringing our skillful mindful awareness to our thoughts in this way is next-level anger management. It is our thoughts that hook in to the body's survival mechanisms to take the anger and run with it. So now we can maintain awareness of those thoughts sufficiently to have more choice over which ones to nurture and turn into intention and action. This is where the rubber meets the road.

PART THREE

YOU CAN CHANGE

This section will attempt to tie together all you have learned about your anger and how to manage it through mindfulness, adding more tools to bring anger management fully into your day-to-day—even your moment-to-moment—life. We'll revisit one of the most important facts: Anger won't ever go away. It's a valuable emotion, after all. We can learn and use the tools to *live* with it and *manage* it in a much healthier way.

CHAPTER 6

Living with Anger

Now that you've learned the core physiological and cognitive systems of anger, you are equipped to deal with your anger in the real world. You are ready to respond instead of react. You **can** respond instead of react. In this chapter you'll learn practices you can do every day to build on what you've learned and create a habit of working through life's challenges instead of being rolled over by them or ensnared by them. In this chapter we'll go over the different life domains of work, love, and family and friends, and learn skills for each.

Feeling the Anger

From the moment we wake up in the morning, anger becomes available. The sound of an alarm at 6:10 a.m.—way too early. Who made the sun so bright? Why do I have to go to work today? Why hasn't my child learned to sleep late yet? Oh man, I forgot to go shopping yesterday, and there are no eggs in the house! Argh, and there's no more coffee either? Why didn't you buy any *$#*@& coffee? It's now 6:15 a.m., and I am already closing in on a state of rage.

Through our use of the Anger Check-in scale, we have seen it is not about the complete elimination of anger. We are not turning you into some kind of impossible spiritual being free of anger, levitating over the problems of the world with a smile. It is not about surgery; it is about meeting situations in a different way with a different attitude born of the knowledge of the workings of our mind and body. To paraphrase the historical Buddha, when I am becoming angry, I know that I am becoming angry. When I am angry, I know that I am angry. When the anger passes, I know the anger passes. You are still going to experience anger in your life. But you will be a step ahead of it. You will know that you are experiencing anger. Just this degree of mindfulness will save you from becoming your anger.

INTEGRATING THE BODY AND MIND

We have gathered and started to utilize a great foundation of wisdom about our body and our mind. We know now that so much of what manifests as anger comes from the parts of our brain that operate below the level of our more human capacities. This brain activity is designed to keep us safe, fed and clothed, connected to attachment figures, and out of the clutches of predators. This energy does not listen to the rational mind for cues. When these parts of the brain send out a message, the body will do whatever these survival parts of the brain tell it to do, regardless of what rational thought might say. This mental and physical energy sends information to the rational mind, and then the rational mind responds if possible.

Sometimes the rational mind can make sense of it and have a reasonable response. When information and memories process correctly, the rational mind can identify the difference between the dilemma of this moment and the body and mind states of the past. When we are not in the habit of settling the body and mind in order to be able to attend to difficult emotions with a sense of balance, a snowball effect occurs in which the current anger locks in to the feelings, sensations, and misguided thoughts of previously experienced states of anger, and each reinforces the other. Our past becomes more concretized, and it in turn makes the manifestations of current anger worse than they were when they started, and so on.

One of the greatest discoveries and contributions that Buddha made to the world of anger management is the idea that thought precedes action. He clearly stated that before doing anything in life, we set an intention. The problem is that sometimes that intention setting is happening below the level of rational thought by the fight or flight system, and so you look at me sideways and I punch you in the face a split second after my lizard brain sets the intention to do so. Buddha recommended mindfulness practice as the antidote to mindless intention setting and to help fully integrate the body and mind.

Our mindfulness of our bodies helps us settle our bodies and take them out of the ongoing fight or flight reactions that drive and feed our anger. Then we can also bring mindfulness to our thoughts in order to see the thoughts that are skillful and useful and those that are not. And now we have the ability to have a conversation with our angry body and mind and come up with new solutions. This is what the integration of body and mind looks like: mindful communication within ourselves to allow for the setting of new intentions.

RESPONDING DIFFERENTLY–NO LONGER JUST REACTING

Now that we have set up the new ground control center for managing our anger, we can set out into the world and speak and act wherever we go with less fear of turning into an accidental rage machine. We have reset the body system through mindful awareness. We have retrained the thought system so that it might have more agency and skillfulness in choosing thoughts and linking thoughts and feelings. We have set up an internal communication system based on mindful awareness where we set and reset the intention to keep our attention on our body states and thoughts. Now we notice our body and mind states arrive, we notice them change, and we notice them leave.

How does this all manifest as responding differently?

It boils down to two words we've already learned: the pause. Everything we have learned has been leading to this. When we don't have the pause, then we are by definition simply reacting. The pause is where all good things reside. It is in the pause that we can stop ourselves from taking an action demanded by the reptile brain that we may later regret. It is in the pause that we can develop insight that can further fuel a more rational response. It is in the pause that we can formulate a new way of responding—a whole new way of speaking and acting.

Anger: It's with Us Every Day

Anger is a normal human emotion. So many people have developed the notion that anger is synonymous only with rage. In fact, rage is just one of a number of synonyms for anger. On our 0 to 10 scale, rage lives on the upper ends of that continuum. And I will go out on a limb here and say that rage itself is a normal human emotion. Each of us has those issues or events or injustices that produce a feeling that leans squarely into that high end of the anger scale. It is normal, and it is human.

Three other things that are uniquely human are the ability to have insight, the ability to make rational decisions and choices, and the ability to apply mindfulness to our body sensations, our emotions, and our thought processes. As we face the reality of our anger every day, we need to honor it and let that part of us know that we are aware of it and able to handle these strong emotions. If we can bring mindfulness to the most powerful of our anger—our rage—then we can work our way down and develop mindfulness of the lesser forms of our anger. And if we are in touch in this way with the variety of manifestations and levels of anger, we can address any and all of them at any time.

If we know that anger will be part of our lives every day, then we can do short- and long-term work to support our efforts. In the short term, we want to have on-the-spot strategies like the ones we have developed with our emergency tips and use of the anger scale to create a pause between feelings, thoughts, and actions. We also want to do the long-range work of continuing to lower our resting anger rate. Since we know that anger will be with us each day, why not seek to make it so that we start at a lower number on the scale? That way we will be less in danger of traveling up the scale into dangerous territory, where we may have less control over our actions.

Using a combination of mindfulness skills that address our in-the-moment struggles and an ongoing program of teaching our body, mind, and spirit to lower our breathing rate, our heart rate, and our blood pressure, we will find ourselves able to live with our partners, our families, our workplaces, our trips to the grocery store, our drives on the freeway–all of our relationships and our daily interactions–while also feeling at peace with ourselves and others.

>>>——➤ Emergency Tip

Exercise is one of the many long-range keys to reducing the resting anger rate. Sometimes we are able to use our long-term strategies in the moment. It may help if you have private space for this one, but perhaps the sight of you dropping down and beginning a set of push-ups might defuse a situation due to its strange nature. Either way, a quick burst of physical activity at a level you are capable of can often work off some angry energy quickly, using up the adrenaline and cortisol anger produces and changing your perspective.

WORKING WITH DAILY TRIGGERS

One of the major mindfulness teachings is the truth of the three characteristics of existence. They can be paraphrased like this: *Things are always changing. Life is often unsatisfactory or difficult. And taking things personally is at its heart illusory as well as painful and unnecessary.* Of course, sometimes when people do things that annoy or anger you, it is based on actions or speech that affects you personally. For our purposes here, let's just say that a large majority of the time, it is actually not personal. One of the best examples of this is a road rage situation. Someone cuts you off on the freeway. A great deal of the rage you feel may come from taking it personally–the belief that the other person knew it was you in the car, they didn't like the make and model of your car, or they actually were able to intuit some personality characteristics about you that they didn't like, so they cut you off. The more likely scenario is that they didn't see you, or they are just a bad driver, or maybe you were going too fast, resulting in the illusion of being cut off.

If you can respond to situations on a regular basis without taking it personally, I guarantee your resting anger rate will improve overnight. There is a saying in Al-Anon, the 12-step program developed for people who have loved ones with an addiction. In that program I have often heard people say, "They're not doing it *to* you. They're just *doing it.*" There will be situations where deeply personal interests will clash and the anger will center on these differences, but if our first inclination is that it's not personal, we will save ourselves a lot of grief and improve our mindful anger management skills exponentially.

⟫➤ MEDITATION: IT'S NOT PERSONAL

Here is an exercise designed to further develop this skill of not taking things personally. We are going to use a modern-day mantra as a tool. As you go throughout your day, notice times when you feel your anger coming up, perhaps as it pertains to little things. For instance, you take that jar of pickles out of the fridge, and you try as hard as you can to twist off the cap because you really, really want a pickle. You struggle and strain and still no pickle. At this point, try saying out loud or silently, "It's not personal." Take a couple of breaths, and maybe even say the mantra again. Then you can resume your work on the pickle jar. You run it under hot water, you dry off the lid, you give it your best grip, and . . . it still won't budge. And now pickles are pretty much the only food on earth that will make you happy. Take a moment and repeat the mantra: "It's not personal." Say it a couple more times while mindfully breathing.

This exercise may give you new perspective on some of the cognitive distortions that feed anger and make things terribly worse. For example, you might think, *This pickle company has it in for me. I can never open pickle jars. Pickles hate me. The entire world is against me.* Notice how anger has less to feed on when these personalized distortions are taken out of the mix. This exercise can be used on more complicated and triggering issues as well.

Anger at Home

Mismanaged anger in the home can be so destructive over time that the world's religions have been grappling with it for millennia. In the Jewish faith, a great deal of emphasis is placed on having peace in the home. The teaching is called *Shalom Bayit.* According to Talmudic teaching, "If one brings peace into the home, it is as though peace were brought to all the people of Israel." There is great resemblance here to the Buddhist teaching of loving-kindness, the many Christian teachings related to loving thy neighbor, and similar teachings throughout worldwide spiritual and religious traditions.

Mismanaged anger can end sibling relationships, it can destroy parent-child bonds, and it can wreak havoc on primary relationships. It can even take extended families and splinter them, sometimes with no resolution. This covers a whole range of territory, from fighting over who gets the remote or who is the favorite child to family members holding grudges and resentments that lead to a literal lifetime of no longer talking. All of these are our concern in building anger management skills for the short, medium, and long term. We want to deal with the small stuff for its own sake and so that it doesn't turn into big stuff, and we want to take care of already entrenched resentments and grudges so that we can have a more pleasant internal and external life with those we are closest to.

WORKING WITH TRIGGERS AT HOME

Sometimes dealing with anger triggers at home can feel like the highest mountain of all to climb. As mentioned earlier, your family knows how to push your buttons because they installed them. In a sense, your household is one big anger trigger waiting to happen. This is not just about the "you always hurt the one you love" syndrome. It's about how intense the implied competition is in a household or extended family for love, attachment, resources, food, clothing, care, and all the rest of our needs. In a relatively happy home, we are successful at providing for all those basic needs that keep people at least at a baseline of some equanimity. At the same time, though, even in a relatively happy home, there is ample opportunity for any one of the people in that home to feel that their needs are not getting met. At that point the anger response becomes important in getting that need met, and, because it can easily go awry, it needs to be managed.

What are some of the triggers people encounter in the home? Well, they are practically endless. Maybe it's bedtime according to the parent and not so much according to the child. Perhaps one parent doesn't like to cook, the other does all the cooking, and resentment builds over time. It could be siblings fighting with each other—the anger response in action—while the parents have two different ideas of discipline, so now everybody is in chaos. One adult sibling could be jealous of the other and act out in aggressive or passive-aggressive ways that lead to an eroding of communication. Perhaps a parent does not approve of someone their child is dating. A child does not approve of someone their single parent is dating. Large and small, the limbic brain and the reptilian brain are always on the lookout for needs not getting met, whether they are only perceived needs or actual needs.

This is where the rubber meets the road across the spectrum of life domains. More than any other trigger, even more than grief and sadness, the greatest bottom-line trigger for anger is perceived or real unmet needs. Whether it is for material things or for a needed value like respect, whether it is a need for a new car or for justice to finally be served in the world, we are constantly on the lookout for our survival. Mismanaged anger over time leads to a greater and greater scope of those people, places, things, and ideas that are perceived as survival needs. This is not to say that some of what we become angry over is not in fact about survival. People with social justice concerns, people angry over their loss of housing or income, people angry regarding any number of actual life-or-death issues—this is our anger addressing real unmet needs, providing the fuel to get our needs met if used wisely. However, the point at which perception of life-or-death needs bleeds into other areas is often where anger takes over the scene, designs the strategies, and leads the parade. We begin that cycle of accidentally bypassing our cognitive abilities in our decision-making—and we may not even know or understand why this is happening.

In the home, everything feels like survival. It is the place we have all agreed to make our survival together our number one goal. If we add solid anger management strategies to the picture, we can learn the art of thriving rather than just surviving.

⟫⟩➤ VISUALIZATION: THE PINK BUBBLE

Here is a mindful visualization that you can use to let go of either ongoing angry feelings or long-standing resentments. First, find a comfortable place to sit or lie down. You may stand if you feel you need that to keep a sense of alertness as you do this visualization.

To begin, see yourself in a very beautiful place, maybe on a mountain, in a field, or at the beach. Let yourself bask for a few moments in the beauty of the place. Then invite the person with whom you are having a problem into the scene. Have them come closer and closer as you smile gently at them, knowing you are in charge of this scene. When they get close enough, put your hands out as if holding a small ball, and then start to expand your hands apart, visualizing a pink bubble growing in between them, much like blowing up a piece of bubble gum. When the bubble is good and large, invite the person into the bubble, and watch them come into it.

Imagine them now weightless within the bubble. Let them know that you are going to let them go now, with love and compassion. Then toss the person in the bubble into the air. Watch them for the very long time it takes the bubble to disappear fully, just like a helium balloon floating up into the sky. When they are completely gone, check in with yourself and see if there are any changes in your body sensations, emotions, or thoughts. Feel free to journal about the experience.

Anger at Work

Many of us spend more waking hours at work or school than we do at home. Work relationships have their own special complications, and work and school present unique stressors that can trigger fight or flight. Lack of work-life balance can lead to exhaustion that can lead to difficulty engaging the rational part of the brain efficiently. That colleague who joined the team after you gets the promotion you were looking for. You love your colleagues, you work well as a team, but your boss is a micromanager and steps in regularly to, well, micromanage. Your company goes bankrupt, and you live on the edge regarding your career. Your job seems like *Groundhog Day*, and you can't find satisfaction in the task or the relationships. Then there's the commute....

WORKING WITH TRIGGERS AT WORK

The element of competition is present at work in a different fashion than at home. We may be in a competitive spirit with ourselves, trying to be the best we can be. We may be wondering if the upcoming layoffs are going to affect us, so we need to rise to the top and not be expendable. We may also find ourselves with personality differences with coworkers. Maybe they are more assertive, and maybe it seems to us that they are more than that: They are aggressive. Perhaps I have a desire to keep work as work, and my coworkers want me to be more social than I like. All of these can raise anger levels, among many other ways that we can be triggered.

There is almost more at stake at work than at home, as this is our livelihood. Working with our triggers can be the difference between employment and unemployment. At work, often it can be hard to find the time and private space to do the work we need to do to manage our anger. So at work we need a combination of self-soothing and communication-based strategies grounded in mindfulness.

⟫⟩→ BREATHING PRACTICE: MINDFUL CHECK-IN

When you are in the workplace, being able to do short mindfulness check-ins is crucial because of the limits of time and sometimes the restrictions in space. Here is a way to work with your breath and body in short form and with the possibility of staying on the down low. Locate a spot just outside your nostrils or just inside your nostrils. If you are stuffed up, use your mouth instead. As you locate that spot, start to notice the quality of your breath—whether it is warm or cold, short or long, deep or shallow. Go ahead and take deeper breaths if possible, each time saying the following to yourself silently: "When I am breathing in, I know I am breathing in. When I am breathing out, I know I am breathing out." If anger is present, you can say, "When I am breathing in, I am breathing in compassion for myself; when I am breathing out, I am releasing my anger." This is not a method of denial or bypassing. It is a method of letting go of on-the-spot anger in order to be able to bring our neocortex back online.

Anger in Intimate Relationships

Back to that idea of "you always hurt the one you love." And back to that idea of what is at stake. In intimate relationships, fear of abandonment or betrayal can bring out some of the worst in us. Those who act out their anger can turn to emotional or physical violence. Those who don't act on the feelings but stuff them down can become mentally, emotionally, or physically ill over time.

Just as with families and in the workplace, there is a never-ending supply of possibility for mismanaged anger in our intimate relationships. Our partner never wants sex or wants it too often. We fight over money. Politics enters into our intimacy, and we lose control of our emotions. Jealousy, whether earned or unearned, can set things on a dangerous course. Our intimate partner acting out their anger in ways we were raised with triggers us, and we respond in kind. Or it can be as simple as one partner wanting to go out to see some comedy and the other wanting to stay in to watch Netflix. How do we work with all these major and minor triggers?

WORKING WITH ANGER IN INTIMATE RELATIONSHIPS

Working with anger in intimate relationships bears a lot of similarities to working on them in the home, especially when we relate it to the homes we grew up in. The 12-step recovery saying "If it's hysterical, it's historical" describes something true about anger in general and about what mindful anger management is really about. Anger management based on mindfulness is about bringing us into the here and now so that the extra special sauce of past difficulty and resentment doesn't enter into the current picture (as much). We are not looking for perfection. But we are looking to heal as much of the past as we can so that we can deal with the anger-making situations of the present with clear vision.

It is clear that past unhealed wounds related to anger will help trigger present situations or exacerbate them at the very least and that acting out (or repressing further) our current anger then reinforces the past memories, which further expands the negative anger web, and on and on endlessly. The very nature of intimacy makes it hard to back up and have any kind of objectivity to take some of the energy out of our anger driven by intimate relationships.

Following is a mindfulness-based communication exercise that you and your partner can use to perhaps heal wounds or at least intervene in current anger loops.

⏩➤ PRACTICE: A MEETING OF TWO

This exercise is about mindful listening. Since our intimate relationships have so much fuel from the limbic brain, where our emotions are based, we may need special times, places, environments, and rules of engagement in order to help each other get our needs met and deal with any angry feelings.

First, set aside a dedicated time for this meeting. Agree that this meeting is designed for each of us to let our partner know what is up for us that could lead to angry reactions. Set a timer for an agreed amount of time, usually 5 to 10 minutes per person. One speaker does all the speaking, and there is no cross talk. The listener just listens to the feelings and thoughts of their partner, uninterrupted for the agreed period of time. At the end of the time, both partners thank each other for their participation, and then they switch roles. Again, there is no cross talk. This is not a dialogue per se; rather, each partner is getting the opportunity to be heard.

For this exercise to work best, it is good to agree to either have time apart after the talk to digest what was heard or not to enter into a dialogue about the material for at least 24 hours or until a couple's therapist is present if the couple is working with one. The purpose of this exercise is to make sure there is as little stuffing of anger as possible in the relationship, as this is the primary cause of blowups—the repressing of anger over time, resulting in a nasty buildup of resentment and frustration that locks into one incident and . . . kaboom. With this exercise, the detonator is taken away over time.

⟫⟩→ TRIGGERING EVENTS MONITOR

Here's your final weekly calendar of triggering events, to track how you're feeling and what you're thinking during the events. Once you complete this chart, look back through your previous charts and notice any progress.

DATE/TIME	TRIGGER	TRIGGER INTENSITY: 0–10	THOUGHTS	ACTIONS	BODY SENSATIONS

Final Thoughts

In this chapter we looked at how we might bring our newfound mindful anger management skills into our day-to-day life. Armed with our education about the mechanics, we can now take a more objective and reasonable approach to our difficulties in work, love, and homelife. We are now well on our way to a more mindful approach to our anger and other strong emotions—not by destroying them or surgically removing them but rather by honoring, understanding, and working with them.

CHAPTER 7

Anger Management for Life

In this chapter, we'll assess where you are on your exploration of your anger, where you still have to go, and what you still want to learn. We will also see what you've learned about what is beneath your anger and what your best tools are to respond to those needs with curiosity and kindness.

Anger Check-in

Check yourself and see where your anger is right now in this moment on a scale of 0 to 10. Notice why you think you are at your current number. Notice if you have found yourself changing over the course of this book and if you have a clearer picture of what your number is on a regular basis.

0   1   2   3   4   5   6   7   8   9   10

Sticking with What Works

Anger management is not cookie-cutter. You need to find what works for you. Mindfulness in general is also not one size fits all. In my over 25 years of teaching mindful anger management, I have grown more and more invested in presenting the both/and approach rather than the either/or. Either/or thinking is actually one of the major triggers for people. When I live in that either/or space, built in to that bottom line attitude is the potential for conflict or disappointment in outcomes. This is not to say that we should not have opinions at all. It means that if we start from a both/and attitude we automatically have more options, and we remove at least some of the conflict from our lives. From this both/and place we can test all the options and choose what works for us.

You have done that throughout your journey with this book. You learned information about the body and mind—some of it new, some of it perhaps review for you. But you learned it through the mindful anger management prism, so that information has new meaning for you now. Based on what you've learned, take a moment to answer the following questions in the space provided.

What is your mindful response to anger raised by on-the-spot situations?

What mindfulness skills are you using to relate differently to long-standing resentments so that they might heal?

What results have you seen regarding the lessening of your general level of anger?

_____

_____

_____

_____

What positive internal resources have you built, resulting in positive mind states that are energized by anger but manifest as something different?

_____

_____

_____

_____

Whatever is bringing you the good results–keep doing that. That is your current anger management prescription.

In the world of medicine and therapy, when we give prescriptions they are based on a treatment plan that is fluid. As my needs and behaviors change, the treatment plan changes, and so does the prescription. Go with what is working for you right now while also staying aware of changes as they come. Perhaps new skills will be needed as you discover more about how you tick, and some skills will become redundant.

Here is an assessment of your current anger management prescription. Go ahead and note what is working for you among all of the tools we have gone over during this journey. It's good to have the list complete, with all that you are not finding useful now, because perhaps in the future you might add to or subtract from it. There is also some blank space for you to note any tools, skills, thought processes, or behaviors that you have found on your own as you went through this workbook.

➤➤➤ WHAT WORKED FOR YOU?

The following list is a partial inventory of the skills you have learned in this book. In the lines following each skill, write a few words about how this particular skill or exercise helped you or did not help you.

Breath counting

_____

_____

Mindfulness of breath

_____

_____

Mindfulness of body

_____

_____

Mindfulness of pleasant/unpleasant/neutral

_____

_____

Daily (or more) anger check-in

_____

_____

Weekly trigger tracker

_____

_____

Counting to 10 (or higher)

_____

_____

Walking away (if possible)

_____

_____

Loving-kindness meditation

_____

_____

It's not personal meditation

_____

_____

Exercise

_____

_____

Study of the workings of the biology of anger

_____

_____

Study of the workings of the cognitive aspects of anger

_____

_____

Yoga

_____

_____

Movement-based mindfulness

_____

_____

Walking meditation (and walking away)

_____

_____

Other tools, skills, thought processes, or behaviors you have found helpful

_____

_____

Over the last 25 years of teaching meditation to people, I have landed on the basic premise that daily practice is more helpful than high quantities of practice on one or two days out of the week. The way we become different in our habits, thinking, and behaviors is through daily repetition.

Five minutes of meditation a day is better than 30 minutes of meditation on Saturday and none the rest of the week. This absolutely applies to anger management as well. Since mismanaged anger is most often caused by untended anger over time that boils over or implodes, it behooves us to cultivate a daily practice utilizing some of the tools we learned in this book. Here is a suggested way to plan your daily practice. Remember that no two people are exactly alike, so make changes where necessary.

Body practice: What is my body-oriented practice? What can I use for 5 to 10 minutes daily to remind me of the different sensations and feeling tones in my body?

Mind practice: What practice will I use to scan and/or change the content of my thinking? What can I use for 5 to 10 minutes daily to remind me of the impermanence of my thinking and the ability I have to use my cognitions wisely to support my anger management strategies?

Heart practice: What practice can I use to bring compassion to my own anger? To the people and situations I am angry with? What can I use for 5 to 10 minutes daily that will keep me in touch with the workings of my heart?

Mind/body/heart practice: What practice can I use to integrate these three sectors? What can I do for 5 to 10 minutes daily that will remind me that I am not a fragmented grouping of elements but someone who can become integrated in my thinking, my body, and my spirit?

Through this simple equation, we have committed to continue just 20 to 40 minutes a day of dedicated work on our mindful anger management skills. Even five minutes a day on one of these will continue the progress. See what you can commit to, and see how you do in the coming weeks in rolling it out.

》》》━━➤ Emergency Tip

What are your ongoing distractions? What distractions lead you down negative pathways? What are you watching for entertainment? What are the news sources you consume? Are you arguing about politics with strangers on social media? See what negative distractions are still in your life, and look into ways to change those patterns. See if you can replace them with positive distractions.

Committing to Yourself

Now let's take a look at how we got here, to this place of healing and growth. You arrived here at the last chapter of this book through a great deal of work and perseverance, faith and courage. Let's go back to the beginning of your journey. Recall the time when you realized you had a problem with your anger. Remember the conversation with a loved one, coworker, or even law enforcement where you realized you would have to change. Remember scanning the Internet (if you did) for resources, and recall finding this book or its recommendation from someone who cared. Remember your purchase of the book and the perhaps mixed feelings as you waited for it to arrive or brought it home from the bookstore.

Take a moment and notice the positive intention that you set by opening the first page of the book. Notice how all of those intentions that you had set up until that point, no matter how tentative, fed the one that had you go to these pages for answers and solutions. Remember the feeling as you signed the statement of commitment to yourself in the introduction. And now remember all the work you have put in. Maybe notice situations that you have been in recently where you responded rather than reacted. Where you let the pause happen. Notice where you have found the time to do your dedicated mindfulness practice and where you have used your mindful anger management tool kit for in-the-moment self-intervention. Notice where you have used it to lower your resting anger rate. Notice any and all of the positive ramifications in your work life, your homelife, and your intimate partnerships. Also notice where you still want to see improvement. And know that you can get there with the same focus and courage that brought you to where you are now.

VALUES

When Buddha laid out his prescription, he did not simply say "focus on your breath and all will be well." His prescription was a comprehensive eightfold path where mindfulness is to be a way of life that infiltrates both our inner and outer worlds. There are three sets of factors comprising this eightfold path: the wisdom factors (wise understanding, wise intention), the ethical factors (wise speech, action, and livelihood), and the mindfulness factors (wise effort, mindfulness, and concentration).

Let's apply these factors to our goal of anger management. The wisdom factors involve having a correct understanding of anger and then being able to set intention from this place of correct understanding. Skipping over to the mindfulness factors, we are encouraged to develop an ongoing effort to be mindful and then to cultivate practices that increase our ability to have focus as well as to achieve nonjudgmental present-time awareness as a way of being in the world. The ethical factors are about what we do in the present moment—we speak, we act, and we live in the world of maintaining our livelihood. Here we are able to utilize all the wisdom and skills acquired in this book and elsewhere to live more peacefully in this world.

When Buddha laid out these teachings, he did so in the context of what he saw as the problem. He saw greed, anger, and delusion robbing us of insight and taking us on a monkey mind journey into those three states of mind. Not only does anger live on its own in that equation, but greed that is unfulfilled and delusion that is confusing can both trigger more anger. Therefore, anger management becomes an incredibly powerful force that can change the course of all of our doings. We relieve ourselves of the acting out of our anger, we are able to generate greater insight, and then we can speak, act, and do our work from a place of clarity and strength.

The bottom-line value that Buddha proposed as a possible binary choice point for our speech, actions, and livelihood was this: Are we being harmful or harmless? Again, looking back to the beginning of our journey, we talked about anger being an energy we can work with to get our needs met or to create change in our world or the world at large. Is my speech harming myself or others when I am in my anger? Are my actions harming myself or others when I do not find a way to bring in my more objective rational mind? Am I allowing my anger to manage my life, or am I managing my anger so I can live in a new way? At this point in our journey, you might see many ways in which you have traded harmful ways of dealing with anger and other strong emotions for harmless methods.

Buddha did not talk about only this one value, nor have generations of spiritual teachers, psychologists, and philosophers. Focusing in on core values and the bigger picture, finding what is important to you, and then gearing efforts in that direction—all of these lead to greater anger management. Sweating the small stuff triggers so much of our anger. When we can take the 30,000-foot view and see what is actually important to us, we can move forward with less of the small stuff in our way.

Following is a mindfulness-based exercise to help you identify the values that drive you and uncover any adjustments that might bring them further into your life.

»»—▶ EXERCISE: VALUES

Take this opportunity to begin looking at what you value. Not everyone
has the same value system. You can use the categories below as a starting place, and you can look more deeply into each of the categories to find
your priorities in life. Use the space beneath the list to write out the top
three areas where you feel you are living in your values and the three areas
where you feel you have some work still to do.

- Family relations
- Marriage/couples/intimate relations
- Parenting
- Friendships/social life
- Career/employment
- Education/personal growth and development
- Recreation/fun/leisure
- Spirituality
- Citizenship/environment/community life
- Health/physical well-being

LIVING MY VALUES   MORE WORK TO DO

On the lines below, make some notes regarding the three value areas where you feel you have some work to do. Start to plan how you might bring them into more focus and list concrete steps you might take to bring them further into your life.

Taking Care of Yourself

For years I have taught anger management as an adjunct of, an aspect of, or a key component of stress management. When we look at the biological makeup of the stress response, it is similar to the anger response. And when we look at the deleterious effects of anger and stress, they match up pretty well. A life lived in an ongoing state of anger or stress can bring physical, emotional, or mental illness. It can bring the end of all spiritual thoughts and feelings. It can keep the mind and body in an endless state of scanning for danger, living in fear, and acting upon those fears on a regular basis.

All of this works both ways, much like the anger of the past feeds the anger of the present and vice versa. How you take care of your mind, body, and spirit affects your anger management, and your anger management (or lack of it) affects your self-care. Taking a proactive and structured approach to taking care of yourself in a general way to manage your stress is a key component of anger management.

STRESS MANAGEMENT

What are some ways to manage stress on a daily basis? There is the age-old admonition to stop and smell the flowers. Earlier in this book we talked about the pause as a way of stopping anger from being acted upon. The pause can also be a proactive resource. How many times a day do we find ourselves with a moment or more where we could take a different view of things and act in minor, subtle ways to bring more happiness to ourselves and others? Stopping and smelling the flowers. Stopping and petting a dog in the street. Smiling at people we transact with at a store. Taking a moment to listen to sounds of the street or the chirping of birds.

And then there are the less subtle ways to manage our stress. Making a commitment to wake up 5 or 10 minutes earlier to relieve some of the stress of getting out the door. Committing to five minutes of mindfulness practice in the morning. Making sure we don't only make our morning routine about getting off to work or school but also make time for human connections with those we live with. Taking regular breaks at work—getting up out of our seat if we work that way and going for a walk, even a short one. Watching funny movies or talking to a funny friend. Exercising in a way that feels fun and sustainable. Reading or writing poetry, or watching movies or shows you've wanted to catch up on. If you have a spiritual or religious life, praying, meditating, or going to a service. All of these and more can be stress reducers. You can write on the lines below a few more of your own stress relief ideas.

_____

_____

_____

_____

REGULATING EMOTION AS A WAY OF LIFE

One complaint many people who are early in their anger management journey share is that they are afraid they will lose their edge. They believe truly that without their anger, they will be run over by everything and everyone. They believe that life will be boring, and they will lose their passion. All of those beliefs are fed by erroneous thinking. They are predicated on the belief that we are going to kill anger, or surgically remove it, or successfully repress it, and destroy with it all other strong emotions and passions.

The truth of the matter is that we are simply taking perfectly human and useful energy and allowing our wonderful human qualities of reason and insight to participate in the dance of our life in a skillful way. Instead of valuing the passions, the emotions, and our perceived strength through anger over our reasoning abilities, we look at the big picture, we look at all three parts of our brain, and we allow them to do what each is best at doing. We allow the reptilian brain to help us jump out of the way of the oncoming car, we let the limbic brain help us navigate survival and ways of thriving, and we let our neocortex, our uniquely human mind, organize and work with all these other aspects to create a way of life more free of the consequences of working without the clarity of insight.

Regulating your emotions as a way of life is not a joy killer. It is not a flatline creator. It is not living in denial. In fact, it is the opposite. By regulating our emotions, we get to harness the more unwieldy ones, and we get to feel the fullness of all our emotions. We also get to use that energy in conjunction with our reasoning abilities in order to do our work, love our loved ones, show up for people in dynamic ways, create works of art, and live in the present moment. As my Zen teacher told me years ago, we get to be fully alive. Reason without emotion is half a life. But so is emotion without reason. And emotion without reason can get dangerous if those emotions tend toward anger. So this job of anger management goes beyond just avoiding the awfulness. It goes beyond just surviving. It has us thriving, living full lives with all our emotions, and doing less harm to ourselves and others.

►►► SELF-REGULATING

Here are some of the ways you can continue on your journey of self-regulating your emotional life to bring you to a place of less stress and less anger:

- Anger check-ins
- Taking mindlessness breaks
- Taking mindfulness breaks
- Daily body practice
- Daily mind practice
- Daily heart practice
- Daily spirit practice
- Assertive, not aggressive, communication
- Daily exercise
- The pause
- Checking in with lowering the resting anger rate
- Knowing what you need and asking for it
- Reframing on a regular basis
- Not sweating the small stuff
- Taking the 30,000-foot view

Final Thoughts

This journey has just begun. In this final chapter we have seen how regulating our emotions does not take the passion out of life but rather puts it in its best place for feeding our life goals. Through practicing what we have learned in this book, our anger is managed, our stress goes down, and our lives become healthier and sweeter. I thank you for having me on this leg of your journey and hope that our paths may cross again some time along the way. Until then, I end this book with some loving-kindness phrases that might guide you as you move ahead: May you be free from fear, may you be healthy, may you be happy, and may you be at ease.

And always remember: Anger is an energy! Use it wisely and compassionately, and you will live well.

Resources

BOOKS

Brach, T. *Radical Acceptance: Embracing Your Life with the Heart of a Buddha.* New York: Bantam Dell, 2003.

Chödrön, P. *Don't Bite the Hook: Finding Freedom from Anger, Resentment, and Other Destructive Emotions.* New York: Random House Audio, 2017.

Chödrön, P. *When Things Fall Apart: Heart Advice for Difficult Times.* Boulder: Shambhala Publications, Inc., 2016.

Coleman, M. *Make Peace with Your Mind: How Mindfulness and Compassion Can Free You from Your Inner Critic.* Novato, CA: New World Library, 2016.

Harris, D. *10% Happier: How I Tamed the Voice in My Head, Reduced Stress Without Losing My Edge, and Found Self-Help That Actually Works—a True Story.* New York: HarperCollins, 2014.

Kabat-Zinn, J. *Full Catastrophe Living: Using the Wisdom of Your Body and Mind to Face Stress, Pain, and Illness* (revised ed.). New York: Bantam Books, 2013.

Levine, S. *A Gradual Awakening.* New York: Anchor Books, 1989.

Nhat Hanh, T. *Anger: Wisdom for Cooling the Flames.* New York: Riverhead Books, 2001.

Salzberg, S. and R. Thurman. *Love Your Enemies: How to Break the Anger Habit & Be a Whole Lot Happier.* Carlsbad, CA: Hay House, Inc., 2013.

Siegel, D. *Mind: A Journey to the Heart of Being Human.* New York: W. W. Norton & Company, Inc., 2017.

WEBSITES

Center for Mindfulness in Medicine, Health Care, and Society (UMASS Medical School)
UMASSMed.edu/cfm

Center for Mindfulness (UC San Diego Health)
Health.UCSD.edu/specialties/mindfulness

The Centre for Mindfulness Studies
MindfulnessStudies.com

PsychCentral Blog: Anger Management
blogs.PsychCentral.com/anger

Mindful Awareness Research Center (UCLA Health)
MARC.UCLA.edu

National Anger Management Association
NAMASS.org

Stephen Dansiger, PsyD, MFT
DrDansiger.com

VIDEOS

Kristin Neff: The Three Components of Self-Compassion
youtu.be/11U0h0DPu7k

What Is Mindfulness? (Jon Kabat-Zinn)
youtu.be/HmEo6RI4Wvs

All It Takes Is 10 Mindful Minutes–Andy Puddicombe (TED Talk)
youtu.be/qzR62JJCMBQ

How to Let Anger Out? (Thich Nhat Hanh)
youtu.be/WTF9xgqLIvI

Tara Brach on Anger: Responding, Not Reacting
youtu.be/jEtNXyYubB0

References

Alcoholics Anonymous. *Alcoholics Anonymous: The Story of How Many Thousands of Men and Women Have Recovered from Alcoholism* (4th ed.). New York: Alcoholics Anonymous World Services, Inc., 2001.

Batchelor, M. *The Spirit of the Buddha*. London: Yale University Press, 2010.

Brach, T. *True Refuge: Finding Peace and Freedom in Your Own Awakened Heart*. New York: Bantam Books, 2013.

Ellis, A. *Reason and Emotion in Psychotherapy: A Comprehensive Method of Treating Human Disturbances*. Secaucus, NJ: Carol Publishing Group, 1994.

Frankl, V. E. *Man's Search for Meaning*. Boston, MA: Beacon Press, 2006.

Gawain, S. *Creative Visualization: Use the Power of Your Imagination to Create What You Want in Your Life*. Novato, CA: Nataraj Publishing, 2002.

Kabat-Zinn, J. *Wherever You Go, There You Are: Mindfulness Meditation in Everyday Life*. New York: Hyperion Books, 1994.

Kübler-Ross, E. and D. Kessler. *On Grief and Grieving: Finding the Meaning of Grief Through the Five Stages of Loss*. New York: Scribner, 2005.

Marich, J. *Trauma Made Simple: Competencies in Assessment, Treatment, and Working with Survivors.* Eau Claire, WI: PESI Publishing & Media, 2014.

Marich, J. and S. Dansiger. *EMDR Therapy and Mindfulness for Trauma-Focused Care.* New York: Springer Publishing Company, 2018.

Maslow, A. H. "A Theory of Human Motivation." *Psychological Review* 50, no. 4(1943): 370–96.

Plutchik, R. *Emotions and Life: Perspectives from Psychology, Biology, and Evolution.* Washington, DC: American Psychological Association, 2003.

Public Image Ltd. "Rise." From *Album*, vinyl. New York: Virgin, 1986.

Salzberg, S. *Loving-Kindness: The Revolutionary Art of Happiness.* Boston: Shambhala Publications, Inc., 1995.

Shapiro, F. *Eye Movement Desensitization and Reprocessing (EMDR) Therapy: Basic Principles, Protocols, and Procedures (3rd ed.).* New York: The Guilford Press, 2017.

Siegel, D. *Mindsight: The New Science of Personal Transformation.* New York: Bantam Books, 2010.

Suzuki, S. *Zen Mind, Beginner's Mind.* Boston: Shambhala Publications, Inc., 2006.

Index

Acknowledgments

There are many people I have met on this path that made this book possible. First of all, I want to thank all the creatives in my life who have inspired me to keep writing. I also want to thank the students of NYC public schools, particularly my students from the early 1990s at Clara Barton High School, who helped me find my voice as a teacher and then my strategies for helping people mindfully manage their anger. Thank you to all my mindfulness teachers, those whom I have sat with in person and those who have touched me through videos, podcasts, and books. A big thank you to all of my clients, colleagues, and friends who have shown me the strength of the human spirit. I would not have finally sat down to put this on paper had the people at Callisto Media not reached out to me, so I thank them for helping me finally share this material. I want to thank my wife and daughter for their support and their patience with me as I met deadlines and talked about anger all the time. Finally, I want to thank the art and punk rock scene in NYC in the late '70s and early '80s–that was where I had my first big taste of the healthy expression of anger, and I tap back into that energy whenever I write, teach, or talk about this subject. Creative expression of the energy of anger has been a lifesaver; for that I am grateful.

About the Author

Dr. Steve played CBGB and Max's Kansas City in the late '70s; drank, played drums in a toy rock band, and then got sober in the late '80s; became an international educator and rocker again in the '90s; and became a sought-after clinician, writer, and meditation teacher in the 2000s. He has taught mindfulness-based anger management for over 25 years as a trainer, educator, and therapist, working in diverse environments spanning pre-K through universities, corporations, government agencies, and mental health agencies. As a frequent guest on Marc Maron's popular *WTF* podcast, Steve has attempted to help Marc with his anger and other issues. He became a master EMDR therapist and provider of EMDR basic training and advanced topics courses as senior faculty with the Institute for Creative Mindfulness and helped set up the premiere Buddhist addictions rehab center, Refuge Recovery Centers. At the center he developed and instituted the MET(T) A Protocol, a design for addictions and mental health agency treatment using Buddhist mindfulness and EMDR therapy as the theoretical orientation and primary clinical practice. He is the author of *Clinical Dharma: A Path for Healers and Helpers* and coauthor (with Dr. Jamie Marich) of *EMDR Therapy and Mindfulness for Trauma-Focused Care*. He avidly blogs and podcasts on topics related to anger management, mental health, recovery, and mindfulness. Besides maintaining a private therapy practice in Los Angeles, he travels internationally, speaking and teaching on mindfulness, anger management, EMDR therapy, the MET(T)A Protocol, trauma, Buddhist approaches to treating addictions, and clinician and caregiver self-care. He has been practicing Buddhist mindfulness for 30 years (including a yearlong residency at a Zen monastery) and teaches dharma classes regularly at meditation centers in Los Angeles and internationally. He lives with his wife and daughter in Los Angeles, California.